PARISH CATECHETICAL MINISTRY

PARISH CATECHETICAL MINISTRY

Rev. Robert J. Hater

Benziger Publishing Company
Encino, California 91316

A resource of the National Conference of Diocesan Directors of Religious Education

Inquiries should be sent to:
Benziger Publishing Company
17337 Ventura Boulevard
Encino, California 91316

Printed in the United States

ISBN 0–02–651130–4

1 2 3 4 5 6 7 8 9 90 89 88 87 86

INTRODUCTION

During the past years, I have become aware of the broad diversity among parishes. While living in different parishes and conducting catechetical programs in my diocese and across the country, I learned that each parish is unique. Local needs vary, and parishes differ in the personal and financial support given to catechetical ministry. As I spoke to parish catechetical ministers, remembered my own parish experiences, served as diocesan director of religious education, and studied the survey of parish religious education directors sponsored by the National Conference of Diocesan Directors of Religious Education (NCDD), it became evident that there is not one but many models for parish catechesis. Considering the diversity of needs, as well as the different sizes and styles of parishes, it is unrealistic to expect, or even to propose, one "best" model for structuring parish catechesis.

If ministry is most effective when people respond out of local needs, then parish catechesis should affirm the individual character of each parish and challenge it to respond to catechetical needs in creative, faith-filled ways. Therefore, I will strive to uncover certain significant issues which apply to every parish. I will also challenge parishes to consider the implications flowing from these issues, in accordance with local needs and possibilities. This book is thus intended for all those engaged in catechetical ministry.

Before proceeding, it is necessary to define the way certain terms are used.

Ministry is participation in the communication of God's love for all people, a love revealed fully in Jesus Christ. Ministry is a response to mission, as mission is directed toward the kingdom of God. The Church exists to evangelize, proclaim, serve, and celebrate the kingdom; thus, the primary focus of ministry is the kingdom, which the Church serves.

One's view of ministry will be affected by one's view of God, church, and kingdom. Related primarily to kingdom, ministry is as broad as evangelization. Therefore, all intentional acts performed by Christians—individually or communally—for the sake of the kingdom (word, worship, service within the family and the marketplace, or ecclesial tasks) are ministry. This view sees the Church incarnating the kingdom through its own ongoing evangelization/conversion process. The focus is primarily on the Church as people of the kingdom, and secondarily on the institution which serves the kingdom.

If, however, ministry is seen primarily in terms of the ecclesial institutional activities (designated church ministries, systematic catechesis, liturgical celebrations), some may prefer to restrict the term *minister* to designated, or official, church ministers.

In this book, *ecclesial minister or ministry* is used for designated church ministers or activities. Taken without qualification, *ministry* refers to the ministry of all Christians, which is coextensive with evangelization.

Evangelization is "the activity whereby the Church proclaims the gospel, so that faith may be aroused, may unfold, and may grow" (*The Evangelization of the Modern World,* 102). In *Evangelii Nuntiandi,* Pope Paul VI states, "For the Church, evangelizing means bringing the Good News into all strata of humanity, and through its influence, transforming humanity from within and making it new" (18). Evangelization is an ongoing conversion process within the Christian community that seeks to initiate people ever more deeply into the mystery of God's love, as it is manifested most fully in the dying and rising of Jesus. This process, inspired by the Spirit, is a response to God's call to proclaim the Good News of the kingdom in word and deed. It is not a separate ministry, but is central to all ministries. It creates the climate for the ministries of word, worship, and service. This approach sees evangelization as part of a lifelong process of conversion in which God's word is heard again and again. This view differs from a fundamentalist kind of evangelization which emphasizes hearing the word of God and accepting Jesus Christ once and for all, in a definitive moment of being converted or saved.

Catechesis further specifies evangelization. It is an element or moment in the evangelization/conversion process. Being a form of the ministry of the word, catechesis "aims at developing an understanding of the mystery of Christ in light of God's word" (*Catechesi Tradendae,* 20). Consequently, catechesis is a process that invites a person to hear, understand, interiorize, and respond to God's word in acts of service and celebration. Catechesis simultaneously strengthens individual faith and deepens involvement in the community. If either of these is lacking, catechesis does not accomplish its full purpose. Catechesis helps families and parish communities (adults, adolescents, and children—individually and communally) to better appreciate and respond to the living Lord, whose presence is discerned in individual and communal experiences, in light of the Scriptures and in solidarity with the believing Church. Therefore, the content of catechesis becomes the lived reality of the risen Lord, as he discloses himself to Christians.

Catechesis, concerned with understanding and transformation, is rich and complex. It can be viewed in a less focused or more focused sense. Used in a less focused sense, catechesis includes pastoral activities—family prayer, speaking of God's love to a friend, community building, evangelizing activities, service projects, liturgy—which, even if not intended primarily to catechize, have a catechetical aspect. In my analysis, I will refer to this usage as "informal catechesis."

Catechesis, used in a more focused way, implies those pastoral activities which aim at calling forth a response to the living word of God in a deliberate, intentional, and structured way. Sometimes, this is called "formal catechesis" or "catechesis proper." Because of certain difficulties with these terms, I use the expression "systematic catechesis." Pope John Paul II describes the aim of systematic catechesis as a "matter of growth, at the level of knowledge and in life, to the seed of faith sown by the Holy Spirit with the initial proclamation and effectively transmitted by baptism" (*Catechesi Tradendae,* 20). Systematic catechesis is directed toward catechizing, which emphasizes understanding, reflection, and transformation. It addresses the whole person and invites the individual to change one's life through listening and responding to God's word.

Liturgy, another element or moment in the evangelization process, is a form of ritualistic action. Religious rituals celebrate the life and values from which faith springs. For Christians, ritualistic action centers in the Paschal Mystery. Within the Christian community, the Spirit discloses the presence of the living Lord, as God continues to offer people the salvation merited by Jesus Christ.

Christian liturgy is the communal celebration of the ongoing dying and rising of Jesus by people who are called together in the Spirit to remember the continued gift of God's love, to engage in repeatable ritualistic action commemorating the Paschal Mystery, and to respond in service to the permanent reality of God's Spirit.

All liturgy acknowledges God's self-manifestation and the community's response in prayer, but not all liturgical celebrations have the same degree of focus or intensity.

The chief liturgical actions are public communal faith responses by the Christian community to the Paschal Mystery. The history and wisdom of the community dictates the form of these liturgical activities, which include the centrality of the eucharistic liturgy, the seven sacraments, or mysteries, of the Christian life, and the Liturgy of the Hours. These focus their dynamism by means of the yearly liturgical cycle. As public manifestations of the Church's fullness, they employ official liturgical rites and are presided over by designated ministers.

Family prayer, public devotions, and other forms of communal prayer also pertain to liturgy. They celebrate the Paschal Mystery in a less comprehensive way.

One further note: With the development of new forms of designated church ministries, it will be important for religious education and catechesis to consider the advantage of beginning to employ a ministerial language now being used in all church documents. This is the language of catechesis, not religious education. Consequently, from this point forward, the language of catechesis will be used. For those choosing to maintain the language of religious education, what is said about catechesis should be translated into religious education language.

No judgment is made about the use of *religious education* in academic and/or scientific circles to include internal criticism, critique of religion or of the Church by religious people, dialogue with other religions that extends beyond denominational lines, and criticism of idolatrous tendencies within the Church itself. Some of these concerns often go beyond the realm of ordinary pastoral catechesis.

Catechetical activity echoes the belief of a faith community, but its nature is not *primarily* to foster a spirit of faithful criticism of the Church itself. The dialectic, however, between the pastoral (catechetical) and the critical (seen both positively and negatively) can be of great value to the Church if carried out with respect and mutual trust, but it can be a disservice if the roles of either side become blurred. It may be useful to specify and legitimize the expression *religious education*, or some such expression, to include the *critical* dimension of ministry in the religious body, and to use *catechesis* to refer primarily, but not exclusively, to the *pastoral* dimension of helping develop an understanding of the mystery of Christ in light of God's word through the community's ongoing initiation of persons into the present state of the Church's faith life, practice, and consciousness. To use the language of catechesis for the pastoral dimension challenges both partners. It challenges the pastoral to be open to the critical and challenges the academic or scientific to be open to the pastoral. In particular, it encourages college and university programs in religious education, religious studies, and catechetical ministry to indicate which programs are primarily pastoral, which are primarily critical, and which are a combination of the two.

This book is a pastoral analysis based on information from theology, ministry, sociology, management development, organization, and education. It is not intended, however, to be an in-depth statistical research study. Many issues that are raised here require further study.

In writing this work, I have attempted to gather as much information as possible from the field, and relate this knowledge to the general trends which seem to flow from recent official church documents. I have not quoted experts on issues raised in this book, although many times I was tempted to do so. I preferred, instead, to rely on church documents and to consult many people from around the country, as this work was in process. I am especially grateful for the suggestions I received from the board members of the National Conference of Diocesan Directors of Religious Education. There are different viewpoints among pastoral, theological, liturgical, and catechetical people about the relationship between evangelization and catechesis, as well as about ways to use terms such as religious education, evangelization, and catechesis. I hope my conclusions provide the basis for further dialogue.

This book proposes no single, all-encompassing model for catechesis in a parish. Instead, it probes key issues, applicable in many different situations. Thus, it is my hope to arrive at a deep level of unity on basic issues, while respecting local diversity. This unity may provide the basis for new directions in the way parishes respond to today's challenges. The book presupposes a "conversion" thrust for all catechesis, and hence, is closely related in spirit to the *Rite of Christian Initiation of Adults* (RCIA) process.

I thank those who critiqued the manuscript and am especially grateful to Sister Susanne Hofweber and Monsignor Thomas Ivory of the NCDD, who gave me valuable advice and support as I prepared and finalized this work. Finally, I thank Joanne Miller and Joanne Beirise who typed the manuscript.

Chapter One

TODAY'S PARISH: NEW CHALLENGES AND OPPORTUNITIES

- ***In the United States, there is a growing trend toward voluntary parishes.***
- ***Each parish develops a vision and style in accord with its own reality.***
- ***The changing context of today's parishes forms the backdrop of parish catechetical ministry.***

The parish exists to help people discover the meaning of the Good News that Jesus proclaimed. His proclamation concerns the kingdom of God. From the beginning of the Christian era, Jesus' disciples gathered together to understand the meaning of that message. Over the centuries, the Christian community has taken different forms, one of which is the parish.

The parish community should be a network of Christian disciples with a common faith tradition, moving toward full realization of the kingdom of God. In reality, most parishes seem to be communities composed of smaller groupings or communities. The parish is meant to live, proclaim, celebrate, and structure the vision of the kingdom of God. How this happens varies from parish to parish, and depends on leadership, community needs and responses, and the cultural and socioeconomic conditions of the times.

History of United States Catholic Parishes

The basic structure of the Catholic parish, since the Council of Trent (1545–1562), is dependent upon sociogeographical groupings, although to varying degrees. Jay Dolan and Jeffrey Burns, in "The Parish in the American Past" (*Parish Ministry* 3, no. 5, 1982), indicate four stages in the history of United States parishes.

Home Parish This parish, common until the end of the eighteenth century, centered Catholic life in the homes of influential Catholics. The family was the basic unit for Catholic education and devotional practice.

Congregational Parish As Catholics grew in numbers, congregations gathered around a central place of worship. The family continued to be a central focus of education and devotion, as did private institutions. Lay people exercised strong leadership. This lasted from the end of the eighteenth century throughout most of the nineteenth century.

Devotional (Organizational) Parish Near the end of the last century, bishops and priests strengthened their control over parishes. At the same time, organizations developed, many new devotions were instituted, and Catholic life became identified with the parish. This type of parish flourished up to Vatican II.

Voluntary Parish Today, the devotional parish, with its strong Catholic identity and loyalty, is changing. People feel more free to choose a parish and determine their degree of involvement. As clerical control lessens, lay people become more involved in parish priorities and ministries. This shift, which is only beginning to be recognized, is having a profound impact on Catholic parish life.

While the Dolan and Burns study indicates a growing trend toward the voluntary approach to parishes, Phase II of the Notre Dame Study of Catholic

Parish Life indicates that "parish boundaries continue to orient the parish life of most U.S. Catholics" (cf. *Origins,* December 27, 1984, p. 465). This study reports that about 15 percent of U.S. Catholics presently cross boundaries in parish selection and about 60 percent cite territorial definition as that aspect which attracts them to their parish. (However, this does not diminish the significance of the more voluntary approach to today's U.S. Catholic parishes, because the study surveyed only registered parishioners.)

Today, the parish remains central to the life of the Church. To be effective, the parish must recognize the inevitability of change and see that it should be "people" gathered together in community, where God's kingdom and presence is proclaimed.

Research points to two critical areas of importance to future catechetical ministry: parish as "people" and the movement toward more voluntary parish participation. Each has far-reaching implications for catechesis.

Many Catholics still consider the parish (or church) as "institution" or "building." They do not regard parish primarily in terms of people. Post–Vatican II catechesis and liturgical practice have helped the Catholic community shift its approach to God and Jesus. In relation to God, the focus has changed from a God of fear to a God of love. In relation to Jesus, the shift from a divine Savior to the human-God has helped Catholics redirect their spiritual life. Today, another challenge looms ahead—to help Catholics acknowledge the parish (or church) as people. This involves more than theology, catechesis, and liturgy. It demands a reorientation of the basic relational structures of the community.

The need for reorientation is underscored by the Catholic trend toward voluntary parish participation. People feel more free not only to choose their parish but also to decide whether to be involved in parish life, whether to switch from the Catholic Church to another denomination, or whether to drop out completely. A significant insight into future parish effectiveness lies in appreciating the profound implications of this trend.

Some people pick and choose "magnet parishes"—those parishes toward which people congregate, often by crossing parish boundaries, because of the quality of parish life and worship—where their needs for spiritual nourishment, wholeness, personal relationships, service, and global awareness are affirmed, nurtured, and encouraged. If this trend grows, the Catholic community will face an entirely new challenge that stretches one's vision of pastoral ministry, including catechesis.

To appreciate the parish as people who increasingly choose their degree of involvement, it helps to look at a parish's style.

A Parish's Attitude, Vision, and Style

The fundamental attitudes of the community affect a parish. These attitudes touch basic levels of human response. For example, before Vatican II, priests and bishops directed the Church, and rules and obligations dictated the Catholic way of life. Today, this is changing. New patterns of belief and action are emerging. These are due, in large part, to the changing role of the laity, especially women, within the Church. The clergy is also affected. No area of church life is exempt from the radical refocusing that is now occurring.

Every family, diocese, and parish operates out of fundamental attitudes. These affect the parish's vision, style, and how communication takes place.

A parish's style reflects a fundamental community attitude and the reason why a particular group responds the way it does. A parish's vision establishes the groundwork for people's interaction. Parishes act out, or celebrate, their vision and life through rituals. For example, the institutional style was ritualized in the many ways the clergy directed the Church. Today, Catholic patterns of morality, church attendance, and parish responsibilities indicate the scope of the changing Catholic vision and life-style.

Changing attitudes present great challenges to parishes. Unlike a pre–Vatican II church, where one style predominated, contemporary parishes represent a variety of attitudes within the same congregation. Avery Dulles uses the categories of *community, service, sacrament,* and *herald* to describe the different styles found in a parish. None of these categories, in itself, is adequate. To avoid conflict and to grow together, people can discover unity in a vision of the kingdom of God, with each person contributing unique gifts to help bring it to completion. Only through trust, dialogue, and mutual understanding and cooperation do parishes recreate themselves.

A group's vision is rooted in the community's interaction. In one parish, this vision reflects an institutional style; in another, it indicates one centered in service or in proclaiming God's word; in still another, a communal approach predominates.

To be faithful to Jesus' vision of the kingdom, parish organizations must model that kingdom with the qualities of love, justice, truth, and righteousness permeating a deep concern for the economically, psychologically, and spiritually poor, as well as an outreach to the alienated and the sinner. The heart of this vision is reconciliation, for the Christian proof for the reality of God's kingdom is the degree of our willingness to forgive.

No two parishes are alike. Consequently, each parish will develop a vision and style in accordance with its own story, ethnic composition, socioeconomic status, size, location, personal and physical resources, and leadership.

The 1982 NCCB report *Parish Life in the United States* discusses various "styles" of parishes today. By *styles* this report means the particular emphasis, or "tone," of a parish, listing the following parish styles:

Organizational This parish, often large in membership, has numerous commissions, meetings, programs, and activities that allow many people to engage in a variety of activities. These are usually active parishes with a significant staff.

Hospitality The tone here helps people to feel welcome or "at home." This style encourages self-initiated activities by parishioners, and does not require any particular formal training or skills.

Formation/evangelization Here, activities focus on issues related to faith. Special emphasis is given to liturgy, sacramental programs, catechesis, retreats, and prayer experiences.

Social action While not limited to poor areas, this style is often found in poorer communities. Emphasis is placed on social services, community development, housing, health, and communal networking.

Service These parishes stress attending to the needs of individual members. Needs may include counseling, support, and various other services. Parishioners are known by name, and the staff is available for parish, home, and hospital visitation.

Culture carriers These national parishes emphasize sustaining the traditions of particular social or ethnic groups.

According to the *Parish Life* report, "there are many other styles and most parishes probably combine two of these styles. The point is that there is no one good style. The style should suit the needs of the people and will be affected by the preferences of the pastor and other leadership" (p. 6).

This report helps one see that the parish vision is ritualized in different styles. Appreciation of the attitudes and needs of people is necessary if an effective organizational model is to be adopted. As the Church reorganized after Vatican II, parishes often established administrative models patterned on business organizations—models which were efficient yet ineffective in grasping the attitudes of the people. Today, the attitude of the group, grounding the vision of the parish, must be considered in developing managerial styles. Parish organization reflects parish vision, not vice versa.

Ministry within the Style and Vision of a Parish

Perhaps the central principle affecting ministry in a parish is that a parish's attitude toward church (as well as toward Jesus and God) will affect its approach to ministry. Often, differing approaches toward ministry are influenced by different perceptions of church. In this context, the pastor's attitude is central; he usually sets the tone that parish life assumes. At the same time, the parishioners influence what happens. They can enhance or block significant renewal efforts.

A critical starting point is the parishioners' views of church. Do they see parish or church primarily as people, or as institution and priests? Do they acknowledge the implications of movements toward voluntary parishes? Parish response to ministerial efforts is determined by parishioners' views of church.

The Changing Context of Parish Life

The changing styles of United States parishes open up new avenues of investigation and new areas of challenge. The *Parish Life* report helps identify the directions effective parishes have taken.

Parishes should acknowledge the personal needs of the people they serve. People today strive for integration and wholeness in order to overcome the fragmentation they often experience. There is the desire to personalize faith. When this does not happen in their parish, many people change parishes or cease active parish involvement. Catholics need opportunities to integrate their enthusiasm into parish life.

Another challenge is to help parishioners address intimacy needs that go beyond those satisfied by family life. Parishes need to address these needs not through the anonymity of structure but through a living message that often may take the form of smaller Christian communities.

The need for wholeness, intimacy, personalized faith, and community are acknowledged by effective parishes. These needs are the starting point for a vision of parish catechesis, liturgy, service projects, specialized ministries to children, youth, adults, and families, parish planning, and hiring staff people.

Parishes should take seriously the four factors of particular significance in parishes, uncovered by the Greeley report, and summarized in *Parish Life.* These factors, in order of importance, are: liturgy and preaching; the need to help people deal with practical concerns, especially those pertaining to their children; democratic or collegial leadership style; and an active quality of parish life.

These confirm the *Parish Life* findings which stress the importance of a team style of leadership, liturgy planning, adult catechesis, youth ministry, and other factors in effective parishes.

Parishes ought to develop the "basics" of Catholic life, while remaining open to adaptation and change. By "basics," we mean good liturgy or prayer experiences, social ministry, and solid catechesis as these relate to parish needs. Without these fundamentals of Catholic life, little deep, long-term parish growth happens. At the same time, effective parishes address the real needs of people and devise creative ways to meet them. A significant insight of the *Parish Life* report is that parish effectiveness depends on how a parish structures its life and ministry, not on its size, location, language, income, or the presence of a school.

Parishes link with the broader community. The parish cannot provide for all the needs of parishioners. It can be a clearinghouse, however, to help people utilize services afforded by government agencies, and to help them network with support systems in the community. In most parishes, the wealth of people's talent and knowledge of available services often goes untapped.

Effective parishes investigate ecumenical possibilities for ministry. Thus, Christian denominations move toward the same goal—the kingdom of God. Keeping this focus in mind, parishes can facilitate a common ministry with other Christian denominations.

Parishes should develop their life and ministry in light of the vision of Church proposed in the *Rite of Christian Initiation of Adults.* The RCIA assumes a parish vision based on the conversion process. This vision implies certain pastoral perspectives—namely, the parish as a ministerial community, people at different faith levels, and a mutuality of ministries.

These perspectives form the backdrop of parish catechetical ministry. It is important to acknowledge that effective parishes have a vision centered on God's kingdom. All parish energies and programs focus on this vision. In this way, there is no room for destructive competition between various parish ministries and activities. In particular, school and parish catechetical ministries are parts of an overall parish vision. If a parish adopts a ministerial model, stressing cooperation in a common mission, parish attitudes are affected. Where this vision is implemented, the building that houses the Catholic school may be considered as a parish ministry center. Then, various ministries—including the Catholic school—would share its use.

Catechesis in Today's Parish

Contemporary catechesis is situated within the vision of a parish such as the one just described. There are common as well as unique aspects of ministry in every parish. The wise minister sees diversity as the opportunity to blend differences within a living synthesis, based on a common approach to ministry and centered on the kingdom of God. Since catechetical ministry specifies ministry itself, conclusions about parish ministry will equally apply to catechesis.

To address effectively the role of catechesis in a parish, it has been necessary to discuss the changing context of parish life. This is where catechesis happens. Now, catechesis will be considered within the framework of the mission of Jesus, the Church, and the parish.

For Further Reflection

1. How would you characterize the attitudes of your parish community?
2. How pronounced is the voluntary approach in your parish? What are the implications this holds for parish catechetical ministry?
3. The report, *Parish Life in the United States,* discusses various styles of parishes today. Which parish style (or combination of styles) best characterizes your parish? What are the implications for ministry in your parish?
4. In what areas of parish life do you see the need for improvement?

Chapter Two

CATECHESIS: THE MISSION OF JESUS AND THE CHURCH

- *The Church's ministry must focus on the kingdom of God. All church activities are measured against Jesus' teaching about the kingdom.*
- *Catechesis is a crucial moment in the evangelization process and is a form of the ministry of the word.*
- *The prophetic calling is rooted in the Christian community. To prophesy is to proclaim the Good News, leading to open and flexible possibilities as opposed to dogmatism or formalism.*
- *The ministries of word, worship, and service ground all specific ecclesial ministries.*

To appreciate the role of catechesis in the parish, it is necessary to relate catechetical ministry to the mission of Jesus and the Church. This is done by situating catechesis within the focus of Jesus' mission and ministry, as continued in the Christian community. This focus aims at the kingdom as the point toward which all ministries converge. In this context, catechetical ministry is specified within the framework of the prophetic call of the Church. The prophetic call, carried out in the parish, is seen in relationship to children, youth, adults (single and married), families, ministerial leaders, catechetical ministers, pastors, and bishops. To understand catechetics in relation to other ministries, it is helpful to develop an adequate philosophy of catechesis that links catechetical ministry to the parish's mission. This philosophy needs to point out the responsibility of the entire Christian community for catechesis.

The Mission and Ministry of Jesus: Challenge for the Christian Community

Jesus was sent to proclaim the Good News of the kingdom (*Lumen Gentium*, 5). Consequently, Jesus' mission was to announce, and bring to fulfillment, this kingdom. His ministry to all people—especially the poor, the sinners, and the alienated—was his response to that mission. His efforts were climaxed in his dying, rising, and sending of the Spirit.

The kingdom Jesus proclaimed is present now, and is still to come. This kingdom, present but not fully realized, exists today in mystery. It is a kingdom where the first are last, and the last, first. The sign of its presence is service—especially to the poor and sinners—and forgiveness. Jesus relates reconciliation with the kingdom because forgiveness is a sign of the degree to which God's kingdom is in our midst.

The Christian community exists to continue Jesus' work. Therefore, the Church's mission and ministry must focus on the kingdom, which is not coextensive with the Church. The Church is not the kingdom, yet the Christian community is intimately related to it. Vatican II recalls the bonds which link Jesus, church, and kingdom: "For the Lord Jesus inaugurated his Church by preaching the Good News, that is, the coming of the kingdom of God, promised over the ages in the Scriptures; the time is fulfilled, and the kingdom of God is at hand" (*Lumen Gentium*, 5). Consequently, all church activities are measured against Jesus' teaching on the kingdom. The Christian community makes little sense if its dynamism and spirit do not reflect the kingdom. To ensure fidelity to Jesus' command, the Church is given the Spirit; the discernment of the Spirit's actions is measured in light of the Scriptures and the tradition of the Christian community.

Sharing the Light of Faith relates the Church's mission and ministry to the kingdom. It says:

> The Church continues the mission of Jesus: prophet, priest, and servant king. Its mission, like his, is essentially one—to bring about God's kingdom—but this one mission has three aspects: proclaiming and teaching God's word, celebrating the sacred mysteries, and serving the people of the world. Corresponding to the three aspects of the Church's mission, and existing to serve it, are three ministries: the ministry of the word, the ministry of worship, and the ministry of service. In saying this, however, it is important to bear in mind that the several elements of the Church's mission are inseparably linked in reality (each includes and implies the others), even though it is possible to study and discuss them separately (30).

The *National Catechetical Directory* uses theological models to describe the mission and ministry of Jesus and the Church when it describes this mission and ministry in terms of word, worship, and service. These ministries cannot be seen in isolation. Neither can catechesis, liturgy, or service projects be classified exclusively and respectively into the categories of word, worship, and service. These ministries interpenetrate each other, although catechesis, liturgy, and service projects may often tend to focus respectively within the general context of the ministries of word, worship, and service. Although these models have limits, the *National Catechetical Directory* recognizes their utility in clarifying aspects of God's revelation and continued communication with people through the mission and ministry of Jesus and the Church.

Catechetical ministry is seen in relation to Jesus' mission and ministry. In speaking of this relationship, *Sharing the Light of Faith* says, "It (catechetical ministry) is a form of the ministry of the word, which proclaims and teaches. It leads to and flows from the ministry of worship, which sanctifies through prayer and sacrament. It supports the ministry of service . . ." (32).

Consequently, the chief focus of parish catechesis is centered in the parish's call to realize God's kingdom. This focus should be reflected in setting priorities, relating to other parish ministries, and maintaining good staff relations. A parish is true to its calling to the degree that its deepest priorities and motivation center on the kingdom. It is worthwhile for a parish to investigate specific ways to flesh out the kingdom of God. The following questions might be helpful in considering a kingdom-centered parish:

1. Are all welcome in the parish—rich, poor, young, old, divorced, single, addicts, gays, disabled people?
2. Is the parish centered on reconciliation and the need to forgive?
3. Does the ministry of the word reflect the spirit of the gospels and help people see how God is present in their lives?
4. Are financial decisions made in light of kingdom needs or in terms of maintenance?
5. Does the parish organizational structure model concern for the poor?
6. Do ecclesial ministers reflect God's presence in dealing with one another and the people?

A sign of how a parish incorporates the kingdom vision is the degree to which it provides catechesis for persons with disabilities. In many places, parishes do little to catechize disabled people. This catechesis is often available only on a regional level, or within the person's family. Each parish has a special responsibility to respond to the catechetical needs of persons with disabilities.

Ministry, Prophetic Calling, and the Church

Parish catechesis must be considered in terms of evangelization and church ministry in light of the prophetic calling—in service to people, in reference to pastors and catechetical leaders, and in union with the bishop and the diocesan catechetical office.

Evangelization, Catechesis, and Church Ministry

Evangelization is the driving force of all church ministries. It is centered in proclaiming the Good News of Jesus' living, dying, rising, and sending of the Spirit. The Paschal Mystery is the focus of all ministry, for the risen Lord continues to bring about God's kingdom through the believing Church. Evangelization is a lifelong process; conversion is being changed by the Good News which evangelization proclaims.

Evangelization gives church ministries a reason and a purpose. In proclaiming the dying and rising of Jesus, which continues in all communal ministry, evangelization energizes Christian endeavors, reminding Christians of their mission to live out God's kingdom. All ministry is rooted in the lifeblood of evangelization; without it, individual or institutional efforts to proclaim the word, celebrate it, or serve others, lack the dynamism promised by the Good News.

A pictorial description illustrates the relationship between evangelization and the ministries that serve the mission of Christ and the Church.

Evangelization, or proclaiming the lived reality of Jesus' dying, rising, and sending of the Spirit, is the marrow of all Christian ministry. It provides the dynamism for the ministries of word, worship and service, which are inseparably linked. In reality, they never exist in isolation, but constantly interpenetrate one another, even though in various church ministries, or at a given time or place, one or the other may

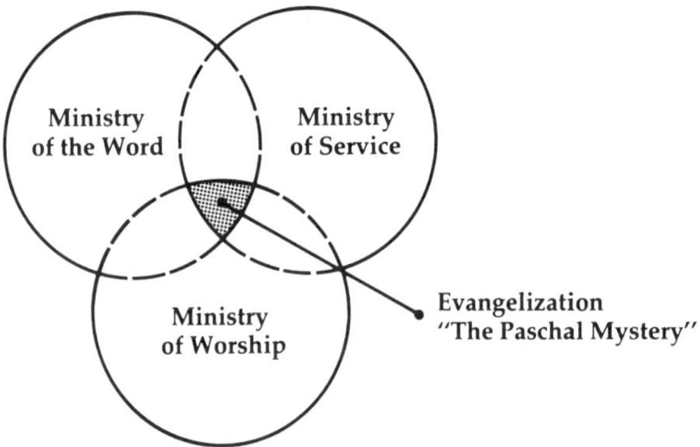

predominate. Their effectiveness depends upon whether or not they are enlivened by the lived reality of an evangelized and evangelizing community.

Evangelization, and its lived reality in a community of word, worship, and service, constitutes the heart of the Church's witness to the presence of Jesus' life, especially manifested in his ongoing dying and rising in the Christian community. All church organizations, structures, and programs exist to help the Christian community evangelize through the ministry of the entire Church.

Consequently, catechesis is seen within the focus of the evangelization/conversion process. *Catechesi Tradendae* relates catechesis to evangelization:

> Evangelization—which has the aim of bringing the Good News to the whole of humanity so that all may live by it—is a rich, complex, and dynamic reality, made up of elements, or one could say moments, that are essential and different from each other, and that must all be kept in view simultaneously. Catechesis is one of these moments—a very remarkable one—in the whole process of evangelization (18).

These words focus catechesis within the dynamic process of evangelization. All church ministries, including the ministry of the word, are elements in the evangelization/conversion process. Catechesis is one form of the ministry of the word. Proclamation of

God's word also happens in preaching, liturgy, and theology.

Evangelization and catechesis are closely related. Although described separately, catechesis cannot exist without evangelization, for its content is the same as the content of evangelization, namely, the person and gospel of Jesus Christ.

Catechesis relates to other pastoral ministries that serve the ministries of word, worship, and service. Each in its own way contributes to the ongoing evangelization/conversion process. A primary responsibility of parish catechetical leaders is to exercise direction, guidance, and leadership in "systematic catechesis." To this end, they utilize every opportunity to see that the catechetical process is the methodology used in all catechetical programs.

Catechesis is closely related to liturgy. The Christian community celebrates liturgically Jesus' ongoing dying, rising, and presence in the family, church, and world. This presence is manifested in life, service, liturgy, and catechesis.

In particular, good liturgy complements good catechesis. As stated in *Sharing the Light of Faith:*

> From its earliest days, the Church has recognized that liturgy and catechesis support each other. Prayer and the sacraments call for informed participants; fruitful participation in catechesis calls for the spiritual enrichment that comes from liturgical participation (36).

Liturgy does not serve catechesis; on the contrary, catechesis encourages a lively and genuine participation in the Church's liturgy. Without effective liturgy to reinforce good catechesis and to celebrate Christian service, the latter efforts are sometimes counterproductive.

Liturgical celebration employs a methodology different from the catechetical process. To develop implicitly a liturgical style patterned on catechesis is a mistake. But this easily happens when a catechetical leader also arranges liturgical functions without the expertise of qualified liturgists. Consequently, effective parishes provide liturgically qualified ministers as well as competent catechetical leaders. When this happens, liturgists and catechists can work together, complementing the gifts these two ministries offer to the wider church community.

The revised *Code of Canon Law* states that catechesis is provided "so that the faith of the faithful becomes living, explicit, and productive through formation in doctrine and the experience of Christian living" (#773). Hence, catechesis is a form of the ministry of the word, intended for people who have heard God's evangelizing word and who have responded with faith. This happens through instruction and the experience of Christian life. The emphasis is formational and holistic. The thrust carries over in the canons on Catholic education, which begin with the responsibilities of parents (#793), and then develop the Church's obligation to help people grow into the full Christian life (#794). Canon 795 stresses that education is holistic, developmental, social, and personal. All church educational systems exist to carry out the basic orientation proposed in these canons that speak of catechesis and Catholic education.

Parish Catechesis and the Prophetic Calling

As a form of the ministry of the word, catechesis is related to the prophetic calling. This calling is present in the history and tradition of both Judaism and Christianity.

Prophecy is intimately linked with witnessing to the kingdom of God. Its presence in the community is a corrective against those human tendencies that often distract people from the call to prepare for God's kingdom.

Prophecy is rooted in the Mosaic covenant. Yahweh, the Holy One, called the Hebrew nation to be a prophetic people. Even though prophecy had various manifestations, only one prophetic calling was given to the Hebrew people. In responding to it, they became a sign of the power of God, as opposed to the power of earthly kings and rulers (Ex 19:3–15; 34:10–28).

Prophecy means "speaking for God." The Jewish people spoke communally for God through their fidelity to Yahweh's call. When they deviated from this call, prophets like Ezekiel and Jeremiah called them back.

In the Hebrew Scriptures, the prophetic calling reminded people that they did not live in a lasting city, but awaited one to come. The messianic hope provided the tension that allowed the Jews in exile to hope for a better life, when grief and oppression would cease. But when the Hebrew people achieved stability, the prophets warned the people to avoid complacency, for the kingdom of God is not of this world.

This prophetic call always recognized the freedom of God, as opposed to the domination or control exercised by human powers. This tension led the prophets steadfastly to oppose a stable, closed outlook on religion or life. The prophets condemned a one-dimensional approach to belief in how God deals with the Hebrew nation. Their message was that people cannot manipulate God; Yahweh is the free God, beyond human comprehension or expectation.

The prophets of the Hebrew nation constantly addressed the word of God and the Hebrew tradition to their current situation. Their voices radically opposed the established religious or social order when that order was not in keeping with Yahweh's intentions. The prophetic voice remained alive because the prophets refused to subjugate God to human powers.

Jesus' challenge to the power of earthly rulers—civic and religious—took a radical shape when he announced his message of forgiveness, healing, and compassion. In the infancy narratives of Matthew and Luke, this challenge begins immediately by contrasting God's power to the power of the king. This continues throughout Jesus' ministry and is particularly evidenced as he exposes the false religiosity of the Pharisees and constantly challenges them to return to the original spirit of Judaism. It was climaxed in his dying and rising to new life. Jesus' resurrection is the eternal reminder of the total freedom of God, and how

God's power can change grief and despair into a new future.

Prophecy, in the Judeo-Christian tradition, is rooted in the community. It was given to the Hebrew people and continues to exist in the community called Church where the risen Lord manifests his prophetic witness in the Christian assembly. This witness speaks of an "event," the Word made flesh, who continues to live in the Church. The ministry of this continuing event—the Word now incarnate in the Church—is basically prophetic. It speaks for God in calling people to relate their stories to the story of Jesus and the kingdom. To prophesy is to proclaim the Good News, to evangelize, to question, to challenge, to be converted through accepting the saving actions of God. All members of the Church are called to witness this saving event; all have a prophetic role. Consequently, to bear witness to Christ in deed or word is to communicate the prophetic word of God.

The entire Church community exercises a prophetic calling. To limit this calling to one or another group within the Church, such as theologians, pastors, or bishops, is just as unacceptable as to claim that institutional church people cannot be prophetic. Both claims are based on too narrow an understanding of prophecy. There are varying dimensions of prophetic witness, and all are legitimate.

Catechesis exercises primarily a prophetic, pastoral dimension in the Church by concentrating on helping to develop an understanding of the mystery of Christ in light of God's word, expressed in the present state of the Church's faith life and practices. At times, other ministries, such as theology or religious education, exercise a prophetic dimension of ministry by fostering a spirit of faithful criticism. They constantly encourage the community to relate the present state of affairs to the Judeo-Christian vision, centered on the biblical notion of the kingdom. The Church is one prophetic community. When various dimensions of the prophetic word are heard, the Spirit remains alive.

Although the prophetic calling is present in the ministerial activities of the entire Church, it is uniquely focused in the ministry of the word where the Good News of God's kingdom is announced. Thus, pastoral ministries responsible for proclaiming this Good News have a special role in ensuring that the prophetic message be heard, both in secular society and in the church community.

Viewing catechetical ministry from the perspective of the prophetic calling allows parish catechetical leaders to see exciting possibilities. First, there is the need to clarify the prophetic calling in catechetical ministry throughout the parish. This means helping people to see that faith is not a fixed, closed system but a journey toward full realization of the kingdom, where God is totally free and will not be manipulated according to human designs. Therefore, the Church has to be open and flexible if it hopes to remain faithful to the prophetic calling of the Hebrew and Christian Scriptures. At times, Christians may be called to question civil society, hierarchical actions, and parish structures when these deviate from God's word and Judeo-Christian tradition.

Next, the prophetic calling encourages catechetical leaders to help parishes and schools incorporate prophetic insights into systematic catechetical activities. Unless the prophetic response permeates the entire catechetical process, catechesis may soon revert to dogmatism or formalism. Catechesis educates for justice and challenges Christians to recognize the idols they have often made of money, power, and success. Catechesis also helps people to see their responsibility for questioning the degree to which these values permeate society.

Finally, if one views the catechetical leader as a servant-leader, an interesting insight into the prophetic role of this ministry is brought to light. The catechetical leader exercises a pastoral role by encouraging the parish to minister and catechize according to the prophetic mode. The servant-leader is sometimes comforting, bringing pastoral service and answering needs as they are perceived. At other times, the servant-leader is challenging, bringing the vision of the kingdom (and the wider church community) to bear on the local community, and calling people to a deeper appreciation of what they ought to be as church. In some cases, the prophetic calling demands that the catechetical leader question the Christian community itself, including its pastors, to ensure that God's word remain alive.

Parish Catechesis and the People

In any parish, the needs of the people should have top priority. In exercising its prophetic calling, the focus of parish catechesis must always be on people—especially families, singles, children, youth, parents, the disabled, catechetical leaders, catechists, religious, and priests. Catechetical leaders should call forth the gifts of the entire community. Consequently, the style of the parish (including its leadership, management, and organizational design) should be structured so that the people served significantly influence the decisions that are made. The style of the parish helps facilitate catechesis by rooting catechesis and catechetical decisions in the people themselves. These decisions, however, are made in creative dialogue with the pastor and with ministers sensitive to the most helpful, up-to-date catechetical processes and materials.

In particular, parish catechesis tries to be sensitive to the needs of families. The term *family* refers to a variety of living situations—integral, nuclear, divorced, single-parent, and others. God is first disclosed in family experiences; as such, the family is the subject of God's evangelizing process. Parish catechesis, rooted in the family, is meant to support and encourage family ministry through supplemental activities and programs.

In stressing the importance of family, the needs of single people cannot be overlooked. Today, parishes are challenged to reach out to single members in an effort to help them hear God's evangelizing word in a way that best suits their state in life.

The Pastor and Catechetical Leaders

According to the revised *Code of Canon Law,* #757, the chief catechetical leader in a parish should be the pastor. One of the pastor's major responsibilities is the ministry of the word carried out as a "servant of the Word," by preaching, by overseeing parish catechetical instruction, by fostering the spirit of the gospels, and by providing an open climate where effective catechesis can happen. The pastor exercises this responsibility in conjunction with other qualified ministers.

Parishes employ different models of catechetical responsibility and leadership. Consequently, the expression *catechetical leader* is a generic expression, indicating anyone responsible for some leadership in parish catechetical ministry. The person could be an administrator of all parish catechetical activities, a master catechist who coordinates catechist formation, or a grade-level chairperson who coordinates catechist inservice, arranges other meetings, and supervises or evaluates catechists. The individual might also be a director of adult catechesis, or the coordinator of youth ministry in its catechetical component, or an RCIA director appointed to oversee catechesis in the catechumenate.

To clarify parish catechetical leadership, it is often helpful to distinguish administration and formation. Some catechetical leaders are excellent at the management level of a parish's catechetical ministry, but may not be as good in the formation of catechists. Others are very gifted in catechist formation, but have neither the ability nor the desire to administer parish catechesis. Although catechetical administration and catechist formation are often centered in one person, sometimes they can be exercised better as distinct ministries—the former referred to as a "catechetical administrator" and the latter as a "master catechist" or "catechist formation director." Consequently, all people involved in parish catechetical leadership are included in the expression *catechetical leader*.

Each parish develops its leadership in relation to the overall style of the people and vision of the parish.

It is important to specify the accountability and responsibilities of all catechetical leaders.

While the revised *Code* emphasizes the pastor's responsibility for catechesis, it also advises him to enlist other Christians to share in catechetical ministry. In this mutually shared ministry, the roles of catechetical leader and catechists are important. Those chosen for these ecclesial ministries should be people of faith, with the knowledge and skills required to catechize in the Catholic tradition, and possessing the personal gifts needed to motivate those being catechized. Parishes need to be careful to select leaders who will have the responsibility for successful parish catechesis.

Good communication must exist between all catechetical leaders in a parish—the pastor, parish catechetical leaders, and those engaged in specialized catechetical ministries, such as ministry to the disabled. It is imperative that the pastor meet regularly with other parish catechetical leaders to give the staff personal incentive, support, and inspiration. If the pastor has the chief responsibility for developing a real passion for catechesis in a parish, he has to live this out in the support he gives to catechetical leaders and catechists.

The Bishop and Diocesan Catechetical Office

The local bishop is called to be a special sign of the presence of the kingdom. He is the chief shepherd of the diocese. As such, the bishop is to be a focal point of evangelizing and catechetical activities.

Vatican II and subsequent church documents establish a close relationship between the bishop, parishes, and diocesan catechetical personnel. Following the directives of the *Decree on Bishops in the Church,* the *General Catechetical Directory* says, "The catechetical office, therefore, which is part of the diocesan curia, is the means which the bishop as head of the community and teacher of doctrine utilizes to direct and moderate all catechetical activities in the diocese" (126). Consequently, those working in the office collaborate in the pastoral ministry of the bishop.

The diocesan catechetical office often works closely with the bishop. In this capacity, the office exercises leadership so that the mission of Jesus and the Church may be realized. The catechetical office justifies itself by serving God's people, keeping before them the message of the Good News. To accomplish this, the office personnel need to be sensitive to the requests of parishes, and develop good managerial styles, which enable the office to facilitate its ministry.

At the same time, parish catechetical leaders and catechists should respect the bishop, follow his leadership, and collaborate with the diocesan catechetical office. When this happens, parishes build strong bonds between themselves and the wider diocesan community, which enriches the quality and scope of catechesis.

A Philosophy of Catechesis

Each parish operates out of some philosophy of catechesis. This needs to be identified and made explicit in order to determine whether it is in accordance with the mission and ministry of Jesus and the Church. It is advisable to formulate this philosophy in a mission statement, and to review periodically parish policies and procedures in light of it. To assist in this effort, the following elements are necessary:

- The goal or purpose of parish catechesis looks toward its mission of proclaiming the Good News of the kingdom.
- The entire parish community is responsible for catechetical ministry.
- Catechists should work together with other pastoral ministers to carry out the mission of Christ and the Church.
- Good catechesis must be sensitive to the particular needs of the parish community and the individuals within it, and work to build up the community of faith.
- Parish catechetical programs ought to acknowledge catechesis as a part of the lifelong conversion

process. (Systematic catechesis links with the real-life situations of people—e.g., youth catechesis and total youth ministry. Priority is given to adult catechesis, while recognizing the need to provide special opportunities for catechesis at times like marriage, divorce, death, and sickness. Finally, there is the need to catechize for justice, with good liturgy and service complementing catechesis.)

- All parish catechesis must employ the catechetical process.
- The Spirit of the risen Lord gives faith; evangelization and catechesis provide the opportunity for conversion to happen.
- All children, youth, and adults have equal rights to benefit from a parish's personnel and finances in the catechetical ministry.
- The parish should be willing to reach beyond its immediate membership and link with other Christian churches to further God's word in the neighborhood and society.
- The parish must give high priority to catechetical ministry. (Many parishes give only lip service to catechesis. In recent years, evidence of this includes cutting back catechetical personnel—especially professionals—reducing the catechetical budget, and growing lethargy about catechetical ministry. This is unfortunate, considering the positive progress made in catechesis after Vatican II. Unless this trend is reversed, the next decade will see growing numbers of unevangelized and nearly illiterate Catholics.)
- Just salaries and benefits should be paid to catechetical personnel, plus an adequate budget for the catechetical program, so as to testify to the parish's catechetical commitment.

Catechesis is part of a larger effort whereby the parish endeavors to proclaim God's kingdom. This kingdom should be announced again and again. A mission statement is one way constantly to remind the parish of this calling.

Catechesis presumes community and strengthens it. *To Teach As Jesus Did* stresses the importance of community as not simply "a concept to be taught but as a reality to be lived" (#23). The kingdom is lived in community. When this happens, ecclesial ministers (including catechists) encourage community building in all of life. This can be done best if people learn what community is by experiencing it.

For Further Reflection

1. What is your understanding of evangelization? Do you see catechesis as a crucial moment in the process of evangelization? How?
2. How is catechesis carried out in your parish? Does it adequately reflect the catechetical process?
3. Is catechesis related to other ministries in your parish? How?
4. Who are the catechetical leaders in your parish? What are their responsibilities? How do they interact with other ministers and with the people?

Chapter Three

SIGNIFICANT ISSUES IN PARISH CATECHESIS

- *The parish builds on the faith initiated in family living. The parish must recognize changing family patterns and wrok situations.*
- *Catechesis must be linked to a person's ongoing need for conversion.*
- *The catechetical process links personal life with the life of the faith community. The process includes human experience, message, reflection/discovery/ integration, and response, and is used by all systematic catechesis.*
- *The primary responsibility of catechetical leaders is catechesis. Leaders and catechists are partners in ministry.*
- *Catechetical leaders must see that catechists are adequately formed.*
- *The catechetical process and materials must be adapted to the needs of each group within the parish.*

Catechesis is seen within the perspective of the parish developed in chapters 1 and 2. More particularly, this means those engaged in parish catechesis should

- develop their ministry, focusing on the parish's mission to proclaim the Good News of the kingdom;

- see catechesis as a specific form of the ministry of the word, relating directly to the ministries of worship and service;
- accept the prophetic dimension of their calling;
- work toward long-range cooperative planning and evaluation with other staff members; and
- acknowledge and foster a relationship with the local bishop and diocesan catechetical office established to carry out parish catechetical responsibilities.

In light of the above, significant issues present themselves for consideration. These are summarized under the following headings: Refocusing Parish Catechesis; Catechetical Leaders and Other Pastoral Ministers; Catechesis and Parish Policies; Responsibility for Catechesis; Parish Style, Vision, and Organizational Models; Priority of Adult Catechesis; Support of Parish Catechetical Leaders and Catechists; Specific Catechetical Issues; and Diocesan Catechetical Offices and Policies.

Refocusing Parish Catechesis

Responsibility for catechesis belongs to the entire parish. Consequently, all parishioners need to be motivated to acknowledge their responsibility for evangelization and catechesis.

Families are the most important communities where evangelization happens. The word of God comes through life itself, especially family life. Evangelization happens through family life (birth, family love, sickness, celebration). Therefore, the family is the "subject" of the evangelization process, inasmuch as God's kingdom (presence) is uniquely manifested here. This is a better perspective for family ministry than to consider the family "out there" to be evangelized by church ministers. This latter attitude tends to regard the family as the "object" of the evangelization process.

The parish reinforces, supports, and builds on the faith initiated in family living. To see the family as the subject of the evangelization/conversion process invites parishes to refocus the direction of parish catechesis. In turn, without family conviction about the importance of parish catechetical activities, the latter may have minimal support and attendance.

Since catechesis should be concerned about ongoing conversion, family catechesis is especially attuned to people's stages of faith. This is equally true of child, youth, and adult catechesis. To act as if a parish community is a homogeneous group of faith-inspired people is to miss the real Spirit who moves individuals to conversion, each according to one's own journey. It is especially recommended that parishes refocus catechetical ministry in light of the *Rite of Christian Initiation of Adults.*

The RCIA emphasizes conversion, which is a personal response to the evangelization process. The Good News of God's love is manifested in birth, innate goodness, human kindness, work, society, and parish. To live is to relate in a variety of ways to this world. God is present in each of these relationships with life, calling humans to completion. In particular, God is disclosed in family, work, society, friends, and church. Each is the subject of the evangelization/conversion process. Consequently, catechesis is vitally involved wherever evangelization happens—in families, at work, with friends, through parish ministry. Each is in relationship.

It is very important for catechetical ministry to acknowledge God's presence in these relationships. The family is rightly called *the domestic church,* not in the sense of a mini-parish but because wherever Christians assemble in the Spirit of the risen Christ, there we have church. No more intimate gathering exists than when loving people profess faith in the living God. Today, emphasis is placed on family ministry; too often, however, these efforts continue to view family as the object, not subject, of the evangelization/conversion process.

In the growing awareness of family ministry, another human dimension is often neglected. It is human work, or labor. John Paul II, in *On Human Labor,* challenges Christians to take a fresh look at work's importance. Expanding on his insights, one can see work in a wider context as the work of the whole person—physical, intellectual, and spiritual. In this sense, the person (being) who works takes precedence over what he or she does (doing). Frequently, the value of a person is overshadowed by emphasis on *what* one does. The efforts of a disabled person, a senior citizen's prayers, a doctor's profession, a parent's sacrifice, and a custodian's work are all human labor. God is present irrespective of whether work is done alone or with others.

The catechist is called to help people acknowledge the value of their work as a Christian vocation and to encourage them to see God as a copartner in their efforts to serve others, regardless of the form human labor takes. At the same time, catechists and other parish ministers need to acknowledge the pressures and tensions put upon people today because of changing work patterns. These may include working parents, "latch-key" children, high-tech jobs, unemployment, social mobility, and lack of security. A recent survey of a middle-income parish in Phoenix indicated that the parishioners felt the parish was doing a good job on family programs for adults and children. Not surprisingly, however, almost no one said the parish was helping people cope with the pressures and ambiguities of the workplace. This need can be addressed through homilies, catechetical formation, support groups, and enrichment sessions. Many Christians feel pressure as questionable moral decisions challenge them at work. These may include the morality of certain medical procedures, business decisions, and social involvements. People need help to cope with the increasing pressures of a complex world.

Evangelization seeks the conversion that addresses the Good News to this kind of world. If catechesis echoes the Good News, it will illumine the God within contemporary families and work situations, and challenge Christians to say No to movements and decisions that are not of the Spirit.

People of all ages and circumstances feel the pressures of modern life. To be effective, new directions are needed in parish catechesis. The traditional Catholic school and parish school of religion (CCD) models have to be redesigned to meet contemporary needs.

Catechetical leaders, especially the pastor, are responsible for initiating and carrying out an overall parish catechetical thrust. Consequently, catechetical leaders should encourage catechesis on all levels of a person's coming to faith. This embraces all forms of pastoral catechesis, including catechesis in Catholic schools.

In particular, parishes need to look at the quality of their systematic catechesis. Parish catechetical personnel are challenged to develop excellence in catechetical ministry by concentrating on that aspect of catechesis for which they have primary responsibility, namely, systematic catechesis employing the catechetical process. While catechists should encourage catechesis in all aspects of church ministry, they are not primarily responsible for all church ministries (for example, liturgy) which have catechetical aspects.

Informal Catechesis

Catechesis begins at home. Parents first teach their children about God through their love, words, prayers, consolation, celebrations, and forgiveness. The family is the chief focus of catechesis. The move away from organizational and devotional parishes spells a return to the family, in ways yet untried and untested.

Parish catechists need to remember the centrality of the family. Pastoral experience and research indicate that parents, family, peers, and significant adults have the most influence on children and youth. Add to these the impact of television, and a realistic picture emerges for the parish catechist. To be effective, parish catechesis takes into account and builds on what is happening in the broader world of family, peers, work, television, and culture.

Informal catechesis is part of the Church's pastoral and missionary activity. Viewing catechesis in this way allows one to see that many church ministries have a catechetical aspect. Sometimes the expression *informal catechesis* is used to refer to them. Informal catechesis means any pastoral activity—family prayer, community building, liturgical service projects, ecumenical activities—which, even if not primarily intended to catechize, has a catechetical aspect. These activities, rooted in evangelizing witness, provide a receptive climate for God's word and prepare for, or complement, systematic catechesis.

Catechetical leaders are to call the community to a deeper appreciation of the catechetical aspect of the Christian life; yet, they are not directly responsible for all informal catechesis. This is the responsibility of the entire parish. But even if not directly responsible, catechetical leaders call parish members to catechize by the witness of their lives and ministry.

Systematic Catechesis

Catechetical leaders must concentrate on developing quality systematic catechesis, employing the catechetical process. The expression *systematic catechesis* refers to catechesis in a more focused sense. It implies those pastoral activities which aim at calling forth a response to the living word of God in a deliberate, intentional, and structured way.

Pope John Paul II alludes to what has been described as systematic catechesis when he states that "catechesis is an education of children, young people, and adults in the faith, which includes especially the teaching of Christian doctrine imparted, generally speaking, in an organic and systematic way, with a view to initiating the hearers into the fullness of Christian life" (*Catechesi Tradendae*, 21). Systematic catechesis builds on informal catechesis, or the many ways that God's word indirectly touches a person.

While systematic catechesis may take place either on an occasional or regular basis, catechesis on a regular basis is essential in order to provide a catechesis which is complete and integral to Christian initiation. This is especially important when nonevangelized people or new Christians are initiated, and when children and youth are catechized. Either occasional or regular catechesis of a more structured variety may be systematic, but there is a tendency to take a more systematic approach to catechesis if it is done on a regular basis. By systematic, I mean catechesis that employs a definite methodology and aims at presenting the entirety of the Christian message in an orderly and sequential manner.

Using the description of the specific character of catechesis which *Catechesi Tradendae* proposes, one can say that systematic catechesis has "the twofold objective of maturing the initial faith and of educating the true disciple of Christ by means of a deeper and more systematic knowledge of the person and message of our Lord Jesus Christ" (19). Thus, two important elements summarize the specific character of systematic catechesis. First, it is didactic, concerned about teaching the word to those ready to listen. Second, it aims at helping God's word mature in the minds and hearts of those being catechized.

Since the journey of faith is lifelong, systematic catechesis must be closely linked with a person's ongoing need for conversion. Systematic catechesis has special application to the family. It includes more than the family's role in catechesis as it relates to the message of the Church. Catechesis to families also teaches people the ways and skills of being church, as church is expressed in the Christian home. In the family, both informal and systematic catechesis should blend into a vibrant experience of the story of Jesus, as this is lived out in the care, customs, and rituals of a faith-filled family. Catechesis to families should be especially sensitive to the brokenness of many families today, and include help and suggestions for single-parent families, the divorced, and/or substitute families. No longer can catechesis to families presume the one model of the nuclear family.

However, there is not only one method or way of doing systematic catechesis. The catechetical process itself may be structured according to different approaches or methods, such as discussions, input sessions, or personal reflections. The elements described previously, which the catechetical process employs, must be included in any approach to systematic catechesis. Catechesis needs to employ widely differing methods; each, however, should include the elements described under the general methodology of the catechetical process.

The *Rite of Christian Initiation of Adults* emphasizes that coming to faith and deepening one's faith involve questioning, learning about the Good News, accepting membership in the Christian community, and deepening the Yes we make to Christ and the Church throughout our lives. Systematic catechesis employs an approach called the "catechetical process." This process is dynamic, ecclesial, interpersonal, biblical, and aims at deepening a person's faith and Christian life. The catechetical process is the general methodology of systematic catechesis.

The catechetical process presumes an ongoing dialogue with the ecclesial community. Jesus, in his teaching, emphasized the close link between the lives of his disciples and the history of the Jewish nation. The Christian catechist is challenged to act in a similar way, by helping those being catechized to appreciate our rich Judeo-Christian heritage, past and present. As this happens, the catechist invites them to learn how they grow and receive strength from the ecclesial community, through appreciating the gifts of others in the parish. This link with the community also leads those being catechized to worship and service.

A person's readiness is a vital factor in the catechetical process. Hence, the catechist is aware of the faith levels of those being catechized, the social, ethnic, and general circumstances affecting them, and how the above-mentioned factors impact on the moment of catechesis.

Systematic catechesis takes various forms, including adult formation, retreats, days of renewal, as well as parish, school, or home settings for child and youth catechesis and lectures. Regardless of its form, systematic catechesis employs four elements of the catechetical process.

Human Experience Catechesis addresses persons in the context of their lives, on the individual's journey of faith, the person's present needs, past experiences, and future aspirations, and utilizing these life experiences as the basis for listening and responding to God's word. Catechesis helps people listen and respond to God's word in light of the teachings of Jesus and the Church.

Message The catechetical process relates the revealed message—the special story of God's dealing with people—to the individual's life story. Here, catechesis shows how the Hebrew and Christian Scriptures, as well as the teachings of the Church, shed light on a person's lived experience. Helpful ways to assist in this process include storytelling, drama or plays, role playing, Scripture study, transparencies, films and filmstrips, questioning, lectures, discussions, and quizzing. The best androgogical and pedagogical techniques and resources available are used. This dimension of the catechetical process aims at teaching and being informative.

Reflection/Discovery/Integration This aspect of the catechetical process leads the person to internalize the message and to see how it changes his or her life if the individual accepts and lives it. As this happens, the catechetical process helps the person understand his or her feelings and reflections about the message, and see the challenges and implications of what is presented. Ways to help a person do this include personal faith sharing, group dynamics, journal keeping, directed reflection, modern parables, and value appreciation methods. This element of catechesis aims at insight, internalization of the message, and ongoing conversion.

Response Finally, the catechetical process invites one to respond to God's word as it affects his or her life. It asks for an honest response to what has been learned. This leads to acts of service and worship. Helpful methods include volunteer service projects as personal, lived responses to the message, communal prayer, liturgical celebrations, creative writing or art, service activities, and the development of new resolutions for one's life.

The catechetical process, with ongoing conversion as its goal, is centered in God's revealed message as it confronts life and invites one to change. Since systematic catechesis happens in community, each element of the catechetical process includes both a personal and a communal response. The latter often affects the former as the risen Lord discloses himself to individuals through the faith of his Body, the Church.

The four elements in the catechetical process are interrelated; systematic catechesis blends them into a vibrant proclamation of the Good News as it speaks to the life situation of individuals or the faith community itself.

Catechetical leaders fulfill their major pastoral responsibility when they take systematic catechesis and the catechetical process as a top priority. Consequently, work with catechists, parish policies, catechist formation, family and adult catechesis, textbook and media selection, and the evaluation of parish programs, center on developing quality systematic catechesis.

Catechetical Leaders and Other Pastoral Ministers

The parish exists to proclaim through word and action Jesus' call to the kingdom. This responsibility includes teaching, celebrating, and serving. The three interlocking ministries of catechesis, liturgy, and service happen in families, parish outreach, Catholic schools, RCIA processes, adult enrichment, youth ministry, ministry to children, and a variety of other parish activities.

To deepen faith, while sharing hospitality or engaging in various parish events, people need ongoing evangelization and catechesis. Thus, informal catechesis pervades a parish's spirit and vision. Catechetical leaders aid community faith growth by acknowledging the entire parish as the place where catechetical ministry happens. Systematic catechesis is a part of, not apart from, the activities of children, youth, and adults.

It is very important that all ministries include a catechetical component. One weakness tends to surface in youth ministry, for example, when the person in charge is involved with every dimension of youth ministry except the catechetical. Instead, the youth minister should address the catechetical component in collaboration with parish catechetical leaders, directly or through other ministers.

This type of integration is facilitated if catechetical leaders and catechists collaborate with other parish ministers, especially the pastor, youth minister, and Catholic school principal. In this cooperative effort, parish ministers acknowledge their common mission to minister in light of the kingdom. In addition, clearly spelled-out job descriptions provide lines of responsibility and accountability. This is necessary to ensure a smooth-running ministerial team.

Catechetical Leaders

The high turnover rate among catechetical personnel, especially catechetical leaders, is widespread. *Catechetical leaders* is used in a broad sense to include full-time or part-time, paid or volunteer, directors or coordinators of religious education and catechesis in a parish or school setting. During the post–Vatican II years, these ecclesial ministers often were given or assumed responsibilities which went beyond the scope of catechetical ministry. Usually, this happened in response to parish needs.

The heavy responsibility placed on parish catechetical leaders not only took a personal toll, it also made it difficult to develop high-quality catechesis. This is not to imply that none emerged; quite the contrary. But it was difficult (if not impossible) to channel enough effort into systematic catechesis when other pastoral needs were also present. Some parish catechetical leaders operated on a maintenance level; others initiated but failed to maintain good catechesis; still others developed quality catechesis. The latter usually happened because the parish limited the scope of catechetical ministry, or employed a sizeable staff.

The experiences of the past suggest that now is the time to reaffirm a catechetical focus and develop quality catechesis. The goal is excellence, not maintenance. To accomplish this, the responsibilities of catechetical personnel may have to be restricted to catechesis. In particular, this means that the parish be especially concerned about two areas of catechetical ministry: that catechesis be developed from early childhood to old age, including catechesis for disabled persons; and that parish catechists concentrate their efforts on developing excellence in systematic catechesis on all levels.

To achieve a unified approach to catechesis, a good model is to have one catechetical leader responsible for all parish policies and activities related to catechesis, including the catechetical aspects of family, school, and youth ministry. Where separate parish ministers carry out aspects of the catechetical ministry, they need to develop a unified approach so as to ensure the unity of purpose and harmony of parish catechesis. It is hard to proclaim Jesus' Good News of unity and peace when people see significant differences of opinion between parish ministers who implement parish catechetical policies.

Small parishes, where the priest and volunteer parish personnel catechize, have a unique opportunity to develop a unified catechetical vision. Perhaps it is easier in closely knit communities for families and friends to acknowledge their responsibility for catechesis. Where there are no professional catechetical personnel, the priest and volunteer catechetical leaders need to see that parish catechesis for all age and faith levels is available to supplement the catechesis that takes place within families.

Parish catechetical leaders offer a pastoral vision of leadership to the wider parish. This vision centers on the Paschal Mystery, for Jesus invites people to join him in furthering the kingdom. Leadership, in light of the Paschal Mystery, means following Jesus' example, including a willingness to be co-ministers with others. This model of leadership then becomes one of partnership in ministry.

Catechetical leaders are to call parishioners to appreciate their responsibilities for catechesis in the home and parish. This means helping people perform their ministry more effectively. Catechetical leaders, however, should concentrate on working with the catechists to improve the quality of catechesis.

Catechetical leaders and catechists are meant to relate as if they are partners in ministry. When this happens, there are no we-they or inferior-superior dichotomies among school and other parish catechetical ministries, or among catechetical leaders, principal, and catechists.

Catechetical leaders should be selected on the basis of their faith, knowledge, skills, ability to communicate, and gifts for calling forth, encouraging, and supporting parish catechists and families. Catechetical leaders are communicators and listeners, people who share the Good News effectively because they know and feel the needs of others. Most dioceses have standards, policies, and procedures for hiring catechetical leaders. The diocese ought to assist in developing a process for the selection of parish and school catechetical leaders which includes observations from the diocesan catechetical staff. In this process, diocesan staff people serve parishes and schools by helping to screen prospective parish catechetical leaders and by encouraging qualified, faith-filled people to exercise catechetical leadership. Cooperation with the diocesan catechetical office, before parish catechetical personnel are hired and commissioned, helps develop a better spirit between the diocesan staff and parish or school leaders. Diocesan staffs should treat parish leaders as partners in ministry, taking the initiative to welcome new catechetical leaders into their ministries, and providing support systems for them.

Parishes should be particularly sensitive to volunteer or part-time catechetical leaders. They perform a vitally important ministry. In many places, even though they do not have the same level of professional preparation as full-time people, they bring to their ministry a wisdom, knowledge, and depth of experience that is the result of many years of service, attendance at diocesan workshops, participation in certification programs, reading, listening to tapes, and the witness of life.

The diocesan catechetical office should encourage and empower capable lay people to become catechetical leaders by helping them to appreciate this ministry, by teaching them the basic principles of education, organization, and management, and by preparing them to do catechist formation in parishes and schools.

The diocesan catechetical office should assist parish catechetical leaders, including ministerial leaders in schools, to work with their own staffs. A diocesan staff should hesitate to do for a parish or school what the people on a local level can do for themselves. A catechetical office may have to hold back ministerial efforts in a certain parish because the office may be doing too much for the parish, or exercises too much control over parish efforts. In some places, the catechetical office will have to provide considerable direct assistance to parishes, such as catechesis for sacramental preparation or parental inservice sessions, because parish personnel are lacking. If a parish, however, has the necessary resources to provide its own pastoral and professional services, the diocesan catechetical office simply encourages and guides these local efforts through regular contact with parish and school catechetical leaders.

Catechetical leaders, both professional and volunteer, operate from a ministerial perspective. They are ministers who are also professionals or volunteers—rather than professionals or volunteers who happen to be ministers. Catechetical leaders should be members of the parish team. If this is not the case, they often feel unsupported and unappreciated.

Parishes have a special responsibility to develop effective catechetical leadership. Diocesan catechetical offices are meant to help parish and school catechetical leaders perform their ministry more effectively. On a diocesan level, this means that regular catechetical sessions and policies help encourage and prepare qualified catechetical leaders.

To assist catechetical leaders, the diocesan catechetical office should

- work out a way to help parishes select catechetical leaders and evaluate their performance;
- develop diocesan programs for the certification of catechists, master catechists, and other catechetical leaders;
- recommend and model a salary scale for catechetical leaders based on background, education, and experience;
- provide sample job descriptions, contracts, and models of working relationships between catechetical leaders and other parish ministers (e.g., school principals);
- maintain regular personal contact with professional and volunteer parish catechetical leaders by providing inservice days for them, by encouraging them to meet for mutual support, and by conducting parish visitations;
- establish a regular system of communication with catechetical leaders, for example, a newsletter or a column in the diocesan newspaper;
- assist catechetical leaders to develop effective catechesis, select books, use media, and systematize a scope and sequence for catechetical processes;
- help catechetical leaders devise the best ways to prepare catechists to fulfill certification standards, where they exist;
- encourage catechetical leaders to develop interparish catechesis by serving as a catalyst;
- support catechetical leaders when they are

challenged by groups in the parish;
- consult parish catechetical leaders, as much as possible, when decisions that affect them are made on a diocesan level. The more parish and school catechetical leaders feel a part of the decision-making process, the more inclined they will be to implement the decisions;
- call upon qualified parish catechetical leaders at times to assist the office staff in conducting workshops, lectures, inservice sessions, and parish consultation.

To further parish catechesis, parish catechetical leaders should

- develop a ministerial style that puts top priority on people's needs, not on organizational demands;
- minimize the number of meetings parish people, especially families, are asked to attend;
- focus catechesis in the family (as *subject* of evangelization) and devise ways to bring families closer together, rather than separate them by requiring too much time away from their homes for parish responsibilities;
- encourage family members to minister together and provide babysitting facilities for parents who want to bring their children while catechizing in the parish or attending meetings;
- prioritize catechetical needs, including the importance of family catechesis and quality catechesis;
- be realistic and take time off to play, pray, and celebrate. No catechetical leader should be expected to work over 40–48 hours per week without added compensation. If catechetical leaders work on weekends or evenings, they should be given time off during the week. Perhaps one of the greatest traps catechetical leaders fall into is the "heresy of action." This leads to ineptness, lack of creativity, and burnout. When catechetical leaders have "no time" for prayer, professional updating, leisure, family, and friends,

something is wrong. This is not the image of the kingdom that Jesus proclaimed;

- develop relational leadership skills rather than those that emerge from a production model. Effectiveness in catechetical ministry is determined by the empowerment of people and not by the number of participants in sessions or pages of paper produced;
- empower catechists through effective catechist preparation and provide ongoing catechist formation through inservice training and other forms of catechetical enrichment;
- plan solid catechesis for all age levels, including topics of study, curriculum guidelines, books, and audiovisuals;
- support catechetical and other parish staff personnel, especially during important moments, such as difficulties in catechetical sessions, home problems, sickness, birthdays, and anniversaries;
- cooperate with the pastor and other ministerial staff;
- assist the diocesan catechetical office, when possible;
- maintain good communication on all levels.

Leadership in Catholic Schools

Parish catechetical leaders should assist schools in their catechetical ministry. The degree of this assistance depends upon the organizational model that exists in the parish. If the primary responsibility for catechesis in the school rests with the principal, school personnel probably relate directly with the principal. Where this is the case, school personnel should also relate closely with parish catechetical leaders, so as to ensure a unified approach to catechesis and catechist preparation in the parish. But if a catechetical leader has the primary responsibility for catechesis in the school, school personnel should work in close conjunction with the catechetical leader. In either case, catechetical leaders are involved in order to ensure a common catechetical direction in the Catholic school and other forms of pastoral catechesis.

The principal is the chief ministerial leader in the school, setting the tone for administrators, teachers, support staff, and students. The term *principal* refers to principals on elementary, junior high, and high school levels. A principal may or may not be the school's catechetical leader.

The catechetical leader in a school is the person who has pastoral and administrative responsibilities for all, or part, of the catechetical program. The principal exercises leadership in seeing that catechesis is central to a school's vision and administrative policies. Often, the principal works with a designated catechetical leader to ensure high-quality catechesis, especially in catechist formation and overall program development and implementation. The person chiefly responsible for catechetical leadership in the school may be the principal or someone designated by him or her, such as the chairperson of an elementary or high school religion department, a parish catechetical leader, or a master catechist in the school.

Since the principal exercises such a vital role in setting the catechetical tone of the school, parish catechetical leaders ought to have regular contact with the principal. Cooperating with the principal, parish catechetical leaders can work to establish policies for catechesis in the school, including catechist certification, required catechetical inservice for Catholic school personnel, catechetical books, hours spent weekly in catechetical sessions, and other matters that improve the quality of catechesis.

Catechesis and Parish Policies

Catechetical leaders and catechists must work closely with the pastor. He is ultimately responsible for parish catechetical policies which are in accord with diocesan catechetical directives.

Parish councils are common in the United States. These are consultative groups, intended to recommend policies. A ministry commission or board, accountable to the parish council, greatly assists catechetical ministry. This commission or board recommends policies for parish ministry pertaining to youth, children, early childhood, and special ministries. These recommendations, which become parish policies when approved by the pastor, should link catechetical, liturgical, and service ministries. A unified ministry commission helps avoid the fragmentation often associated with separate catechetical, liturgical, and school boards. If a parish has the latter boards, they should exist to implement the policy directives of the ministry commission within specific areas, such as liturgy, parish catechesis, and the Catholic school. Catechesis must be a high priority of every parish ministry commission.

Some parishes choose to establish a separate catechetical board or commission. Unless integrated under the broader umbrella of a parish ministry commission, this model may isolate catechesis from other ministerial activities. More preferable is the option where catechesis is central to all parish ministry activities.

A major responsibility of a ministry commission is to establish catechetical policies. The pastor works with such a commission to serve the catechetical needs of parishioners. Liturgists, school principal, catechetical leaders, and other parish ministerial leaders are *ex officio,* nonvoting members. Voting members of the commission include people from various segments of the parish.

The ministry commission accepts policy suggestions from the parish staff and other parishioners, formulates needed policy statements, and monitors and evaluates the implementation of these policies. In addition, the commission oversees parish ministry planning, budgeting, and hiring. It is important, however, that the commission limit itself to the general area of policy. The board, responsible for parish catechetical policies, should ensure that this ministry is carried out for, by, and with the people. Grassroot suggestions and observations provide valuable assistance in setting the tone for catechesis in the parish. The decisions of the board are subject to the acceptance of the pastor. Catechetical leaders, liturgists, school principal, and other parish ministers administer catechetical policies. Parishes facilitate ministry by making clear who establishes policies and who administers them.

Responsibility for Catechesis

The answer to the question, Who is chiefly responsible for catechesis?, will be affected by one's view of church. If church is seen primarily as a community or organization, the answer will probably be the *pastor*. While the revised *Code of Canon Law* answers in this way, it significantly shifts the perspective of the 1917 Code, where parish was defined primarily in terms of territorial location. The revised Code describes the parish in terms of people, as a "definite community of the Christian faithful established on a stable basis within a particular church; the pastoral care is entrusted to a pastor as its own shepherd under the authority of the diocesan bishop" (#515).

This description emphasizes the pastor's responsibility for all ecclesial pastoral ministry, including systematic catechesis. Other ministers, including catechetical leaders and catechists, assist in this effort. The key is the pastor. He can be seen, metaphorically, as holding the cork in a bottle. He can remove the cork and gently guide the gifts of the Spirit as they pour forth and nourish new life, or he can keep it in, never allowing the gifts for ministry to overflow and enrich others. When a pastor blocks ministerial efforts, other parish personnel can do little to instill life. If they try without his cooperation, personal jealousy, threats, division, and frustration often result. On the other hand, a pastor who sees his ministry as calling forth, guiding, and celebrating the parish gifts creates a life-giving environment. In this context, catechetical leaders and catechists use their creativity and skills to further the ministry of God's word.

Catechetical ministers ought to know the actual parish situation before beginning or continuing this ministry. The time has arrived to demand accountability of pastors. Without this, unhealthy situations continue, people leave parishes, and other ministers are hurt.

If church is seen primarily as people (family, friends, individual members) united in a Christian assembly through common faith and ritual, the chief responsibility for at least informal catechesis rests with the people, under the guidance of the pastor. The stable community the revised Code defines as a parish consists of families where life originates and is nourished through joy and pain, love and hurt. God's presence is first manifested in life itself; consequently, parents are primarily responsible for introducing the meaning of Jesus' dying, rising, and sending of the Spirit to family members in word and deed.

The trust, compassion, and forgiveness that families teach are basic in the development of human life. Families are the soil in which Jesus' Good News is planted and nourished, for his message confirms the best life instincts. To catechize in a Christian way is to teach that Jesus' message shows us how to live a fully human life. Seen from this vantage point, a primary and lasting responsibility for catechesis rests with the family, especially parents.

Catechetical leaders are bridges between the family and the wider parish community. They receive their commission to teach from the parish as this is confirmed by the pastor. Their call requires special compassion for people. Their priorities center on individuals and families, not the institution. Whenever institutional needs overshadow those of God's people, the work of God will be stifled. If not remedied, the very people who call us to serve will suffer.

Catechists have a special ministry to the wider parish community. They prepare for this important ministry by study, prayer, attending catechist formation sessions, developing skills, and cooperating with parents, catechetical leaders, and the pastor. The catechist has a special responsibility for the catechized. No one should embark on this ministry without faith, preparation, and skills. It may be better to have no systematic parish catechesis than to expose people to poor, untrained catechists who can do more harm than good by turning people off to the word of God and the Church's living tradition. Catechetical leaders, including pastors, have a special duty to see that catechists are prepared.

Catechist formation is ongoing. All catechists need to participate in workshops, seminars, and courses, as well as to read books, journals, and other literature that contribute to their spiritual, catechetical, and theological enrichment. This means parishes should give financial and personal support to help catechists deepen their faith and improve their ministerial skills.

Parish Style, Vision, and Organizational Models

All parish administrators, especially pastors, are responsible for establishing a type of administration that sees the kingdom of God as its goal. Every parish organization or activity directly or indirectly exists to further the mission and ministry of Christ. A powerful influence is often exercised by athletic clubs, social groups, housekeepers, and bookkeepers. If negative, this influence can stifle parish ministers. How tragic when real parish ministry is blocked by a parish organization or individuals who exert undue influence on the pastor or other parish minister! To minister in terms of the kingdom there must be general consensus from the parish ministerial team, or pastor and advisors, as to real parish priorities. Stressing the pastoral approach is not to disparage the importance of parish policies or rules; the latter can become strong support statements to ensure the carrying out of the Church's pastoral mission.

The parish staff ought never leave people with the impression that they are dealing with a big bureaucracy. Catechetical leaders need to remember that the driving force of the Christian community is the Spirit, who is never totally captured in any organizational model. This is not to downplay the importance of good administration. Administration is necessary to identify, call forth, organize, and support the gifts of the community so that "church" can happen. Hence, good management, organization, and planning help fulfill the reason and purpose for the parish's existence, namely, to bring God's kingdom to life and fulfillment. Without competent management and organization, good ideas may never get off the drawing board, and parishioners may experience a high level of frustration.

A pastoral spirit should permeate every good catechetical program, for the pastoral dimension of the Church's ministry is intimately linked to catechesis.

Every parish projects a certain image. With this in mind, catechetical leaders frequently ask whether their primary image is pastoral, that is, truly interested in addressing people's needs through the service they provide and the policies they develop. Where this pastoral image is present, the catechetical staff is usually in close communication with people. Catechetical leaders also regularly evaluate their managerial and organizational approach so as to ensure an adequate blend of pastoral and administrative skills. Both administration and pastoral spirit are important, but without the latter, the former has little impact on moving hearts to appreciate the Good News of God's kingdom.

Parish Organizational Models

Effective administrative and organizational models for catechesis flow from the overall style of parish life. Consequently, no single model for catechetical organization is possible. What works in a rural Kansas parish may fail in suburban Atlanta or inner-city Chicago. What remains constant, however, is the vision of the kingdom. With this, any administrative structure sensitive to parish style gives life; without it, a parish is little more than a social agency or meeting house.

When considering parish organization, certain issues are significant.

- The pastor is central in parish ministerial efforts. He works with parish personnel to inspire a Christian spirit in the community. In a sense, he is the "keeper of the parish vision" and should embody this in his person and actions.
- The pastor has frequent contact with the parish staff, especially those responsible for the ministries of catechesis, liturgy, and service.
- All parish activities and organizations exist to further the pastoral mission of Christ and the Church. Consequently, a pastoral orientation is necessary throughout the parish.
- Finance, building, and athletic committees are meant to serve the chief ministries of the Church, not vice versa. The mission of the parish must influence the way money is spent and personnel used. Without a clear vision of parish needs and priorities, the mission of the parish can be easily overshadowed by money and personnel.

It is impossible to suggest one model for parish catechesis. Parishes vary in style and tone, size and composition. They range from large to small, rich to poor, some having abundant personnel, others suffering from lack of personnel. As a result of varying circumstances and ministerial needs, parish catechesis is organized differently from place to place. It is important, in any case, for the catechetical organization to be consistent with the style of the parish. Otherwise, conflict, tension, and hurt result. If the style of a parish changes, catechetical personnel often cannot shift catechetical direction on their own. This requires the combined efforts of pastor, important leaders, and parishioners.

Rather than suggest parish organizational models, a pastoral perspective will be presented which is operative in any viable model. Utilizing this perspective, a parish can accommodate or change its organizational structures—if changes are in order.

Pastoral Perspective

From a pastoral point of view, the ministries of word, worship, and service are intimately related. The pastor has the chief responsibility for seeing that these ministries are living and active in the parish. Those responsible for these ecclesial ministries ought to be an integral part of the parish staff. Together with the pastor, these ministers set the tone for the pastor's mission, carried out in light of the kingdom.

Specific ministries in a parish staff will vary, depending on the parish's size, location, and needs. Consequently, each parish will adapt the specific ministries (not shaded in the following model) to its unique circumstances. In all parishes, however, the ministries of word, worship, and service (shaded in the model) ground and energize all specific ecclesial ministries.

The leaders—chiefly responsible for the ministries of word, worship, and service—relate directly to each other. These include the pastor and those chosen to implement the parish mission, such as the catechetical leader, school principal, youth minister, liturgist, deacon, pastoral associate, and others. Catechetical leaders administer all catechesis in the parish, including overseeing catechesis in the school,

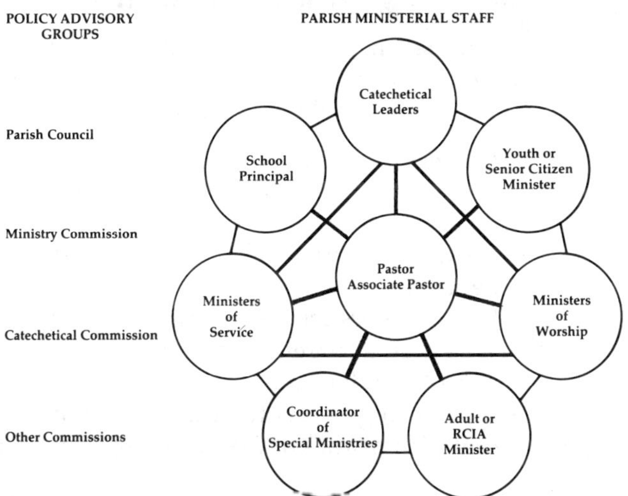

youth ministry, and adult formation, in cooperation with the appropriate administrators of each ministry.

The ministries of word, worship, and service (not money or personnel) must be the focus of parish priorities. Decisions about building upkeep, new activities, or continuance of a school are to be made in light of a parish's mission. For this reason, parish finance officers are not voting members of a parish council. The chief ministerial activities—catechesis, liturgy, and service—are represented on the parish council, ministry commission, and/or catechetical commission by the appropriate ministerial leaders. These leaders are *ex officio*, nonvoting members. People selected as voting members of these representative bodies should be knowledgeable of and sensitive to the parish's mission statement and committed to its implementation. Destructive politics and personal agendas are never appropriate.

The ministries of word, worship, and service are essential to every aspect of parish life. They need to permeate, for example, early childhood through senior citizens' programs. The parish as a whole cannot effectively respond to these ministries unless staff members work together. If catechetical leaders collaborate with musicians, liturgists, and social ministers, parish ministry is strengthened.

Refocusing Parish Administration

Every parish needs to look at organizational structures in light of its mission to realize the kingdom. In doing this, the following are helpful:

- Parishes ascertain their real needs and make decisions based on the attitudes of the people and the vision of the gospel message.
- Needs are prioritized before making organizational decisions.
- Parish leaders ask whether the parish's vision and style need to be refocused in light of the people's attitudes and needs.
- A parish organization centers its vision on the central ministries of word, worship, and service.

- Parishes select ministers who are comfortable with the style and vision of the community. In larger parishes, it may be advisable for a pastoral associate, besides the pastor, to oversee all ecclesial ministries.
- Pastoral ministers, including the pastor, meet often for support and good communication.
- The parish council or ministry commission set the tone for a parish's vision. To do this, the members know their responsibilities, are prepared for their ministry, and attempt to embody the parish vision in their decisions.
- Catechetical style, leadership, and structure are consistent with the overall parish vision.
- Catechetical leaders are responsible for the implementation of catechetical policies.
- Catechetical personnel work closely with parish staff people who are responsible for the ministries of worship and service. Together, people from these three ministries work with children, youth, adults, families, schools, and specialized ministries. To do this, a parish may form individual ministerial teams representing the catechetical, liturgical, and service dimensions of the Church's ministry. There should be good working relations with all parish ministers and organizations, especially with the Catholic school. The school principal also serves on the parish ministerial staff.
- All catechetical activities (Catholic school, adult, youth, and children) incorporate not only catechesis but also liturgy and service ministries. All parish programs include the overall catechetical, liturgical, and service policies and directives of the parish.

Priority of Adult Catechesis

Many parishes are still child-centered, sometimes evidenced in the strong support of Catholic schools and the serious neglect of other pastoral programs. While children's catechesis is critical, church catechetical documents since Vatican II have emphasized the priority of adult religious education and catechesis.

The need and importance of adult catechesis is confirmed by the renewed life that the RCIA gives to parishes. This process presupposes adult conversion. Similar to the RCIA in orientation are other plans for parish renewal such as RENEW. These are adult-centered, emphasizing God's presence in a person's story. The community focus supports and encourages the renewal process.

Adult catechesis is ongoing and rooted in formation, not pure information. Information workshops and lectures are not sufficient. Adult catechesis, based on evangelization, employs the catechetical process, which relates the Christian story to a person's story and invites the individual to new levels of integration, discovery, and response.

The report *Parish Life in the United States* confirms the value of adult religious education and catechesis. In surveying "effective parishes," a question was asked about what programs were organized and involved significant staff time. Number one on the list was religious adult education. In effective parishes (compared with overall parishes in the United States), adult religious education rated 93 percent, compared to 63 percent for general parish practice.

There is no single model for effective adult education, but successful efforts appeal to the needs of adults and take seriously their stories and input. The best content for adult catechesis is related to the experience of the people.

Adult catechesis takes various forms and incorporates the best insights of contemporary adult learning theory. The catechetical leader performs a great service by encouraging parishes to see the central role that ministry to adults plays in today's church. Parish leaders can suggest or initiate a variety of ways to enhance adult catechesis, including parish sessions during the day, businesspersons' sessions in work situations, lectures, workshops, weekend renewal processes (involving adult groups from parishes or schools), retreats, and many more. The parish makes information about these available to interested parties.

Support

If a parish expects catechetical leaders to give effective catechetical leadership, it must provide adequate personnel and resources. Understaffed catechetical leaders cannot prepare catechists, develop curriculum, serve people's needs, manage catechetical efforts, and develop policies. The degree of parish support is often measured by the personnel and resources provided.

Catechetical leaders and catechists need two kinds of support: professional and personal. The first includes financial support, good working conditions, adequate salary and benefits, necessary secretarial assistance, and the audiovisuals to carry out responsible leadership in parish catechetical ministry. Without professional support, little long-range vision may be developed or implemented. Parishes are challenged to reexamine the resources provided for catechists, in light of the suggestions for quality catechesis described in *Sharing the Light of Faith.* Professional support should be aimed at supplying what is necessary for good vision and development, and at paying a just wage and providing adequate benefits to parish catechetical personnel.

While financial support is important, personal support is more important. Most catechetical personnel minister on a parish level because they are convinced of the importance of developing good catechesis in the parish. They often receive personal support from the parishioners, but they also need that support on an administrative level to cope with the challenges and frustrations that are an inevitable part of parish catechetical ministry. This means support from the pastor, parish staff, bishop, diocesan catechetical staff, school office, and other diocesan offices, especially in those instances where parish catechetical personnel are faced with problems which arise in catechetical situations.

Personal support is especially important when working conditions are not good, and when people question the teachings of catechists on doctrinal matters. If the latter happens, it must be presumed that the catechist is correct, unless the opposite is clear. Personal support means trusting catechetical personnel. Because of the volume of words spoken by catechetical people in lectures, workshops, seminars, and private conversations, certain matters may be misunderstood or misquoted. Since no one is perfect, catechists will make mistakes. Unless this becomes a pattern, it ought not lead to lack of support.

If the pastor, school principal, other parish ministers, and catechetical personnel have close communications and good working relationships, support is natural. They know one another. When problems arise, support follows naturally from these relationships. Hence, regular interaction between the pastor, other parish ministers, and catechetical personnel is very important.

Parish catechetical personnel need the reciprocal support of the diocesan catechetical office just as the latter needs the support of the parish. If good communication exists between them, this support usually follows.

The diocesan catechetical office also needs the support of pastors, catechetical leaders, and principals. If an office develops a ministerial spirit of service to parishes, these people usually support it. Then the office receives parish support, because it supports the parish in what the parish is trying to accomplish on a local level.

Finally, parish catechetical personnel need mutual support. Usually, the quality of this support surfaces from the kind of relationships that people have with each other. The experiences of many parishes have shown that two extremes need to be avoided. First, a catechetical staff is not a group of individuals working separately on projects with little or no contact with the rest of the parish staff. This leads to isolation and lack of common purpose. Second, a catechetical staff is not a primary support group. By *primary support group,* I mean those relationships from which people receive their primary psychological and spiritual support. Examples of this might be religious communities, family, or small prayer groups.

While needing to support each other, pray and work together, like a small Christian community, a parish catechetical staff is primarily a goal or task oriented group. It does not exist chiefly for in-depth personal support, as a family does. A catechetical staff is better described in terms of a team, working to achieve a common goal or purpose. The team needs mutual support and encouragement to achieve its purpose and to stand by one another when difficult times arise. If the support takes on the aspect of a primary support group, personal and professional dynamics often get mixed up and the main purpose of the staff is lost.

Every parish catechetical staff needs to look at its ministry in light of professional and personal support, for what it accomplishes largely results from the support it gets on the parish level. If support is lacking, parish staff people find it difficult to maintain their ministry. Support is a needed prerequisite for ministering in an incarnational church. People need one another for strength, especially in times of failure, sorrow, and disappointment.

Specific Catechetical Issues

A high priority in parish ministry should be given to the quality of catechetical leaders, catechists, and catechetical programs. People set the tone for the spirit of Jesus' message concerning the reign of God. Consequently, to improve the overall quality of catechesis, leadership and preparation take top priority. Then, other important issues follow, including family and adult catechesis, catechetical process development, topics of study and curriculum guidelines, books and other resource materials, media, and program evaluation.

Formation

Catechist formation is seen from a ministerial point of view, and not from the vantage point of making people meet certain standards. It is a way to help catechetical leaders and catechists fulfill their ministry, if they are to be effective catechists. When catechesis is seen as a ministry—a vocation—the requirements for this ministry become necessary steps to prepare oneself for serving God's people.

The National Conference of Diocesan Directors of Religious Education has published a useful document entitled "A Study of Catechist Formation Programs." This document emphasizes the importance of faith development, while stressing also theological content and skill development. It refers to the formational elements of catechetical programs as "those which are designed to develop personal faith as well as each of the specific qualities and competencies that enable the catechist to place theological content at the service of effective catechesis" (p. 1). Catechetical formation, consequently, helps catechists mature in faith and express their belief in daily life.

Catechetical leaders must see that catechists fulfill diocesan formation requirements. For this to happen, office personnel and catechetical leaders work in close contact.

A diocesan catechetical office establishes criteria for catechist formation based on a ministerial model. The office also makes available content descriptions of the required courses. Finally, the office sees that ample opportunities are available for catechists to receive the necessary training in the catechetical process and coursework. When courses, fulfilling catechetical needs, are provided on a college or university level, in various parishes or regional centers, or by religious communities, diocesan catechetical personnel should communicate these opportunities to parishes and schools. Where opportunities for catechetical training do not exist, catechetical offices may have to provide these themselves, or work with parish catechetical leaders to help the latter provide them.

If a time priority is necessary, it favors the preparation of catechists. When a parish has well-trained catechists, other catechetical needs usually take care of themselves. Without adequate catechist preparation, the best topics of study, curriculum guidelines, books, media, or evaluative tools are not very effective.

The pastor has the final responsibility to see that catechetical leaders are qualified. They, in turn, are responsible for catechist formation, which is possibly the most important aspect of successful parish catechesis.

Family and Adult Catechesis

Family and adult catechesis are top parish priorities. Family catechesis takes into account the wide diversity of families today. Each parish develops its catechetical processes in light of the family as the subject of evangelization.

Sharing the Light of Faith stresses the importance of adult catechesis:

> While aiming to enrich the faith life of individuals at their particular stages of development, every form of catechesis is oriented in some way to the catechesis of adults, who are capable of a full response to God's word (18).

Each parish ought to address the particular needs of adults. These vary depending on ethnic composition, socioeconomic status, and the particular pressures of a given region. In particular, today's parishes need to address the situation of adults who may be broken through divorce, death, or loss of employment. Family situations enhance or inhibit effective adult catechesis, as do the increased responsibilities and pressures of work and job mobility. Successful adult catechesis develops vision and direction depending on the various circumstances that influence adults. The word of God is addressed to the real situation of adults to give them wisdom and insight into their life's meaning at a given time and place.

The changing situation of adults demands that parish adult catechesis constantly be open to evaluation and revision.

Process Development

Systematic catechesis is most successful when it employs some form of the catechetical process. As described before, this process includes four elements: human experience, message, insight, and response. It is important to realize that there is no single "best method" when using the catechetical process. Successful catechesis varies from catechist to catechist, from group to group. People are different, and what is a good approach for one catechist may not work for another. Methodologies are affected by different cultures, age groups, personal sensitivities, and attitudes. In one instance, it may be better to begin by sharing personal experiences, and then listen and apply the Christian message. In another, a catechist may prefer to present the Christian message and then invite those present to apply it to their lives. In still another, the catechist may leave the application to each person's private reflections. Effective catechesis will be influenced by a person's age and maturity.

Adults often respond well to catechetical processes that emphasize some form of shared experience. The expression *shared experience* refers to any methodology that employs a personal sharing of knowledge and experience. When the content of adult catechesis includes the people's stories, they often see in a deeper way God's presence in their lives.

Not all adults, however, respond positively to sharing their thoughts, attitudes, and feelings in catechetical sessions. An effective catechist is sensitive to the group or individual, employing a method that respects each person. If a shared experience approach is employed with people not comfortable with this method, they may stop coming to the sessions. Consequently, no single catechetical method is employed across the board in adult catechesis.

Adolescents and children also need to see how the Christian story relates to their personal story. Hence, the catechist devises ways to help them understand and appreciate God's word. It is very important that they learn the Christian message, according to their age and ability to comprehend.

Children and adolescents cannot respond to a shared experience method in the same way as adults. Often, young people spend about three minutes discussing an issue that adults talk about for one half hour. In addition, many youth are too insecure or shy to share personal experiences. Peer pressure is strong at this age.

While sharing personal stories may help some youth in their catechetical journey, catechists also need to provide good, short content sessions. In these sessions, catechists teach basic Catholic doctrine, Scripture, morality, and social justice while catechizing youth to appreciate the sacraments, especially the eucharistic liturgy. This catechesis can effectively employ audiovisuals, television programs, archetypal stories, and guided readings. Youth need to learn the Christian message and Catholic tradition. It is necessary in any "conversion" model of catechesis to provide the "ground" in which to root a young person's own story. This does not imply a return to the catechism method. It does imply, however, that catechesis is more than personal sharing, and questions the wisdom of never changing catechetical methodology in children's or youth catechesis.

Young people learn the basics of the Catholic Christian story in order to appreciate their own story. Hence, catechists present the Christian message in such a way that young people learn who Jesus is, what "church" means, and why they are challenged to live good lives and celebrate their faith in prayer and liturgy. This means reading, study, prayer, liturgical and social response, and hard work for young people and catechists alike.

Parents are the primary catechists of preschool children. This catechesis is largely informal, flowing from the natural dealings of parents with children at home, during recreation, or with friends. At this age, children learn values, including religious ones, almost by osmosis. Television has a significant impact on their attitudes.

Parish catechists help parents appreciate how children grow religiously. The attention span of preschool children is short; their experiences are in a state of flux. Consequently, formalized sharing sessions with them may have questionable long-range value. A creative, loving, accepting, and forgiving environment is important in evangelizing young children. In this setting they learn, quickly and gently, simple Christian beliefs and practices—Jesus, God, Mary, prayer, devotions, compassion, and forgiveness. This happens in families and church settings.

People and circumstances are too complex to canonize one catechetical process. Catechists are most effective when they creatively address the needs and situations of those being catechized. Too much emphasis on the catechism method held back catechists before Vatican II; an uncritical canonization of one method today could do the same.

Topics of Study and Curriculum Guidelines

Parish catechetical leaders develop topics of study and curriculum guidelines with specific outlines for early childhood, elementary, secondary, and adult catechesis, as well as catechesis for disabled persons. These are uniform to ensure consistency from group to group, yet flexible enough to allow for diversity arising from different catechetical texts, geographical locations, socioeconomic or ethnic backgrounds, family settings, school, and other parish activities.

These topics of study and curriculum guidelines should be based on the conversion-faith development thrust of the RCIA rather than a school model of education. As the RCIA process takes hold in parishes, it is important to utilize its dynamic to revitalize all parish catechesis. For this to have long-term effectiveness, good planning is necessary. This means clearly defined topics of study (e.g., the Mass, Business Ethics, Growing Together as a Christian Family, Jesus, Sacraments, Prayer, and many more). Regular and systematic catechetical formation, following a curriculum guideline, helps ensure a complete catechesis of essential elements of faith development.

In developing topics of study and curriculum guidelines, catechetical leaders take into account the age and circumstances of those being catechized. Great flexibility is needed, especially in adult and family catechesis. The ethnic and personal background of the participants often dictates the most helpful method to use.

Topics of study and curriculum guidelines provide broad catechetical objectives which give direction to catechists who work in systematic catechesis. They allow catechists to plan lessons in light of horizontal or integrated development (scope) as well as in light of vertical or progressive development (sequence) of the overall catechetical thrust of a parish.

The aim of these instruments is to give the catechist objective norms and identifiable, measurable objectives for catechizing. In so doing, the catechist is assisted in short- and long-range lesson planning, periodic evaluation, and accountability. The topics of study and curriculum guidelines stress the importance of conveying the integral message of Jesus in light of the Church's teaching, by employing the catechetical process.

Books and Other Resource Materials

Parish catechetical leaders exercise responsible leadership in making available the best catechetical materials to catechetical personnel. They provide recommendations and advice on catechetical books and auxiliary text materials, in addition to information on audiovisual materials, such as films, filmstrips, and videocassettes.

Catechetical texts are especially important for good catechesis. The approval of catechetical texts is no simple matter. Since the time shortly after Vatican II, when great differences existed among texts, various series are now coming more closely together in content and format. But in many cases, fundamental differences still exist in their methodology and content. Any texts which are selected should be adequate in content, catechetical process, style, and language. In addition, they ought to allow for parental participation and provide excellent, usable catechist manuals.

Responsibility for recommending catechetical texts often rests with the diocesan catechetical office. In recommending or not recommending various series, the strengths and weaknesses of each series should be stated. These are then conveyed to parish catechetical leaders who in turn initiate a process to decide which series will be used in a particular parish.

Each parish is different; therefore, parishes select different series according to their particular needs. In deciding which series to use, a pastoral approach is followed, mindful of where the parish is catechetically and mindful also of the catechists who must use the books. What may be a valuable series for more qualified catechists may be almost impossible for beginning catechists to use. The catechetical office assists parishes to ensure that the texts chosen best suit the individual parish situation.

A degree of subjectivity is necessary in catechetical text selection; a catechetical office respects this in the parishes it serves. Parish catechetical personnel ought to plan ahead so that books are used for some years, thus eliminating the confusion resulting from frequent text changes. The latter often disturbs catechists, causes undue work for catechetical leaders, and prevents students from developing consistency in their learning patterns.

In the final analysis, while catechetical texts are important, the person of the catechist is *more* important. An excellent book in the hands of a poor catechist will never accomplish what an excellent catechist can do.

Use of Media

Good films, filmstrips, tapes, and cassettes greatly enhance a catechetical lesson. Audiovisuals are effective aids in catechesis to the degree that they are incorporated within an overall catechetical plan. They serve as excellent discussion starters, and bring new insights and motivation to catechesis. *Sharing the Light of Faith* emphasizes this in saying that people "need to grow in their ability to evaluate television and other contemporary media by critical standards which include gospel values" (22). Parish catechetical leaders assist catechists by encouraging media literacy, by recommending the best audiovisuals available, and by providing a lending library of media resources. They also arrange periodic inservice workshops to show catechists the most effective and intelligent ways to use modern media.

Program Evaluation

The diocesan catechetical office makes instruments available to evaluate parish and school catechesis. These instruments give suggestions for different kinds of evaluation, such as program and personnel, formal and informal, and parish and diocesan evaluations. In addition, these tools spell out recommended procedures and include norms to evaluate catechetical leaders, catechists, and parish catechesis itself. The evaluation process is the primary responsibility of parish and school catechetical leaders, and is implemented with the intention of bettering overall parish catechesis.

Catechetical evaluation stresses the quality of the catechists—their preparation, skills, and effectiveness—as well as the leadership of the catechetical leader. No instrument is comprehensive enough to include criteria for evaluating all facets of parish or school catechesis. In preparing for an evaluation, a self-study team reviews significant aspects of parish catechesis, prioritizes their relative importance, and decides which need evaluation. In a parish, this evaluation takes into account the responsibility to provide catechetical opportunities for all people—young and old. Special emphasis is placed on adult catechesis.

Sometimes parish or school evaluation is greatly assisted by inviting input from outside catechetical leaders, including the catechetical office. The latter provides models that suggest ways to invite others to help in parish or school evaluations.

Program evaluation is necessary. A parish ought to formulate a policy requiring periodic evaluation of all parish catechesis.

Parish catechetical leaders agree upon parish catechetical priorities and develop an effective managerial process to meet these responsibilities. In the final analysis, the pastor, catechetical leaders, and catechists exist for the people. Their needs can never be forgotten.

The parish is part of the wider local church. As such, it cooperates with other parishes and diocesan ministers, especially the bishop.

Diocesan Offices and Policies

All catechetical documents after Vatican II emphasize the bishop's responsibility for catechesis and the importance of the catechetical office. *Sharing the Light of Faith* says, "The bishop directs catechesis through the diocesan offices responsible for catechetical activities" (218). To accomplish this, the bishop chooses competent personnel, with a special emphasis on faith, ability to communicate, professional skills, and pastoral sensitivity.

The catechetical office does not make catechetical policies for the diocese; rather, the office recommends policies to the bishop and advises on policy suggestions coming from other sources. In addition, the diocesan catechetical office helps to facilitate and implement policies which are recommended by a diocesan ministerial commission or board and accepted by the bishop. The commission is the people's voice and represents the various constituencies within the diocese. Policies and administrative actions should recognize and acknowledge the needs, wishes, and gifts of the Christian community, especially those of parishes and schools. Once policies are accepted, the catechetical office supports and helps to administer the implementation of these policies.

The policy commission may take different forms. In one diocese, it may be a commission responsible for all diocesan educational and catechetical policies. In another diocese, a separate catechetical commission may exist. In still another diocese, this may be a ministry commission with responsibilities for formulating policies for catechetical, liturgical, and service ministries. This model avoids the fragmentation often associated with separate catechetical, liturgical, social action, and school boards. The latter boards may be necessary in specific areas of competence, but each in its own way can implement policy directives established by an umbrella diocesan ministry commission.

The form a commission takes will be influenced by the diocesan administrative model. Whatever its form, the relationship between the commission, bishop, catechetical office, parishes, and schools ought to be clearly spelled out and understood.

Consequently, people in the diocese, through their representatives on the commission, recommend policies. When the bishop accepts the decisions of the commission, they become policies for the diocese. The catechetical office also recommends policies and helps parents, catechetical leaders, priests, and catechists to implement and evaluate these policies, as the latter groups minister directly to people in parishes or schools. This process respects all concerned and acknowledges the entire people as the people of God.

Diocesan catechetical policies and administrative actions emphasize that the chief thrust of diocesan catechetical ministry is directed toward improving catechesis on a parish or school level. These policies place the major responsibility for the implementation of catechetical policies on the local level. In so doing, these policies strengthen the local catechetical community, for they shy away from centralizing too much authority for catechetical ministry in the catechetical office.

In opting for a pastoral approach, a catechetical office assumes a heavy responsibility. No catechetical office is expected to handle directly all diocesan catechetical needs. There is a way, however, for the office to facilitate catechesis, which places considerable responsibility on local catechetical leaders. This option concentrates on working with catechetical leaders. If a catechetical office works directly with catechetical leaders, the time and talent of the staff will usually be put to better use than if the staff tries to serve every need that surfaces, to conduct sessions that parishes should do themselves, or to work directly with catechists. The office's effectiveness in working with catechetical leaders is influenced by the good working relationships the office has with pastors and priests. Developing good communication and a positive spirit with them is vital.

The parish facilitates its ministry by using the talent and resources of the diocesan catechetical office. Often, resources not available in individual parishes are provided by diocesan catechetical offices.

For Further Reflection

1. Does your parish give priority to adult catechesis? What about family catechesis? Are any areas or groups neglected in your parish catechetical program?
2. Is there a close working relationship between the catechetical leader(s) and the parish school principal?
3. Do you feel it necessary to refocus your parish's organizational model in light of linking together the ministries of word, worship, and service?
4. What steps are being taken to provide adequate formation for catechetical leaders and catechists so as to ensure that they know the basic teachings of the Church and are comfortable with the catechetical program?
5. Has your parish taken seriously the need for good catechetical texts and audiovisual materials? Is there an evaluation of your parish's catechetical program?

Chapter Four

IMPLICATIONS FOR CATECHESIS

- ***The parish catechetical vision is based on reality, namely, the needs, resources, and personnel in the parish.***
- ***There is the need for clarification of the language of catechesis in relation to religious education.***
- ***Evangelization should be seen from a dialogical perspective, the three poles being world, family, and parish.***
- ***Parish as community, as "people," must ground the vision of catechesis, just as all ministry in a parish must be rooted in a sense of "welcome."***
- ***Parish catechetical ministry must return to the simple message of the Gospel.***

Certain implications, flowing from the major thrust of this book, challenge the parish to catechize in light of the kingdom of God.

Parish Composition

No two parishes are alike. This diversity must be acknowledged if catechesis is to speak to church members. To be effective, catechesis reflects the ways that actual parishioners live, for parish ministry helps people better appreciate the kingdom of God in real-life situations.

The kingdom is the focal point for all believers, individually and collectively. A parish is seen in light of the kingdom. Consequently, the structures that facilitate the church's operation serve the kingdom, thereby furthering the life and movement of the Spirit.

Each parish reflects a basic attitude and proclaims the kingdom in the way it lives and acts. A parish is an organic whole composed of people who in their own way respond to the call of the Spirit. Each parish has its unique history, local color, special needs, styles of operation, talent, and responsibilities. Since catechetical ministry is one part of parish ministry, the basic attitude of the parish affects the way the kingdom is proclaimed.

In every parish, the following factors are especially important for effective proclamation of God's kingdom:

- **Acknowledge parish diversity.** This means what works in one parish may not be successful in another.
- **Build a vision on real parish needs.** This vision grounds catechetical ministry.
- **Give people higher priority** than money, organization, or meetings.
- **See the close interconnection between catechesis, liturgy, and service ministries.** This means linking these ministries effectively in any parish model.
- **Recognize the importance of the pastor's role and that of the catechetical leader and catechists** in effective catechesis.

Catechetical personnel cooperate with other parish ministers. Cooperation is greatly facilitated by personal and professional communication. To enhance good communication, parishes should avoid the temptation to overstructure. A basic structure is sufficient. When special needs arise, they can be handled cooperatively by the parish ministry staff.

Catechetical ministers proclaim the kingdom most effectively in an atmosphere where they call themselves and other parish ministers to a deeper level of awareness and cooperation. This atmosphere is greatly facilitated by parish organizational structures that show clear areas of responsibility and accountability. These are needed in catechetical ministry to indicate individual responsibilities. Often, catechetical leaders need to clarify their relationship with school personnel and other parish ministers.

Each parish develops a catechetical vision which takes into account parish needs, resources, and personnel while emphasizing ministry to families and ministry in the marketplace.

The Quality of Parish Catechetical Personnel

Pastor The pastor is a vital factor in shaping parish catechesis. His attitude influences the kind of catechesis that emerges, the parish's priority for catechesis, and the type of ministers selected to be catechetical leaders and catechists.

The pastor has a serious responsibility to see that good catechesis happens in the parish. If the pastor facilitates catechetical ministry in a life-giving way, he should be affirmed; if he fails in this effort, he should be challenged. Because of the importance of parish catechesis, diocesan officials—including the bishop—should know the feelings of parishioners before new pastors or associates are assigned.

The fundamental attitude of the pastor influences the type of people hired and those who volunteer to minister on the parish level. If a pastor encourages people to grow in a common vision of the kingdom, by stressing the pastoral dimension of ministry, people with creativity and/or the desire to exercise pastoral leadership are likely to serve in parish catechesis. If, however, the pastor allows little room for innovation or pastoral sensitivity, this attitude affects the staying power and morale of catechetical personnel.

Catechetical Leaders The spirit of parish catechesis is greatly influenced by the catechetical leaders.

There is no single model for this ministry, but faith, a degree of creative openness, and the ability to manage are useful.

Every leader learns from others. This is especially true in the Church, where the Spirit of God is present in the entire community. Hence, catechetical leaders who allow the Spirit to direct parish catechesis through the insights and creativity of the staff usually create a happy, productive atmosphere. This type of leader blends the creativity of the group into a manageable synthesis. In this context, consensual decision making may be desirable, even if the method of arriving at consensus differs from leader to leader.

A parish catechetical leader needs personal, pastoral, and professional qualifications. Consequently, the individual is a person of faith who communicates this faith to others. This requires pastoral experience in the form of prior ministry in parishes and schools, and professional qualifications, ideally a master's degree in theology, religious education, or contemporary catechesis. To inspire others to carry out the mission and ministry of parish catechesis, the catechetical leader needs to be knowledgeable of basic Catholic teachings and able to communicate them, as well as capable of working well with others, especially with the pastor and parish ministers. Finally, the catechetical leader should be experienced in teaching catechesis, working with parents, developing catechetical curriculum, and have knowledge of good catechetical texts as well as book selection procedures, and competence in using audiovisuals.

Good management is necessary to translate the message of the kingdom into organizational practice. To accomplish this, the catechetical leader must be constantly aware of the vision of parish catechesis in order to fulfill Jesus' mission of proclaiming the Good News of the kingdom. This requires being a person-centered manager, putting people's needs above organizational demands. This type of leader supports the staff, is available to assist and counsel them, and takes the lead in helping the parish formulate a good mission statement and philosophy of parish catechesis, parish catechetical policies, and the goals, objectives, and strategies needed to carry out these policies. All these formulations flow from the needs of the parish and the capabilities of the parish staff.

Catechists Catechists must be prepared. If a parish concentrates on one aspect of catechesis, it should be catechist preparation. Catechists are the key to effective parish catechesis.

Past experience shows that parishes that take catechist formation seriously find better-prepared catechists and a more stable group of catechists. There is much less turnover, because catechists have made a considerable investment of their time and take pride in what they do.

Sharing the Light of Faith describes the catechist's ministry as response to a call from the Lord through the Church to give one's talent and time to catechize others and to continue growing in faith and understanding. Catechists live out their faith in Jesus by sharing it with enthusiasm and hope. They also believe in the Church they represent and strive to foster community. Genuine appreciation of Christian community leads catechists to serve others.

When catechists are vibrant, creative, and knowledgeable people, with the faith and skills to communicate the Christian message, parish catechesis bears fruit. Many people, especially the youth, stop attending catechetical sessions because of the poor quality of catechesis, claiming that it is "boring," that they "learn nothing new," and that "it does not speak to life." People need to be challenged; if catechesis does this, they will usually respond.

Time is at a premium today. To ensure people's attendance at catechetical sessions, the latter must be well organized, have good content, and be directed by faith-filled, compassionate catechists in a way that addresses the needs of those attending.

It is better to take the time to prepare catechists than to offer catechetical sessions with ill-prepared, boring catechists. Catechesis is more than fun and games. People who experience the latter do not receive the motivation instilled by the living word of God, brought alive by a good catechist.

The Language of Catechesis

If catechesis is the chief focus of parish religious instruction, it may be advisable for dioceses and parishes to consider replacing the language of religious education (e.g., Office of Religious Education, Director of Religious Education) with appropriate catechetical language on all levels of church ministry and organization (e.g., Diocesan Catechetical Office, Catechetical Leader). I suggest this because "religious education" is closely associated with a school model of learning. The word *education* carries overtones which can imply learning religion as a person learns mathematics and English. *Catechesis* is process-oriented, and fits better with the current emphasis on conversion as central to pastoral ministry.

Religious educators have struggled for years to clarify the terminology of religious education. In spite of these efforts, there is no common agreement about its meaning today. In addition, even though "religious education" was used widely in the United States, it was not preferred by *Sharing the Light of Faith.*

Official church documents, preferring the term *catechesis* for this form of ministry, set the direction for the future. If religious education terminology continues to be used, it may never be adequately clarified. This is said for two reasons. First, because church documents, now employing the language of catechesis, do not feed into the process of clarifying the language of religious education. Second, continued use of religious education and catechesis adds to the already existing confusion, because in employing both languages, catechists deal with some aspects of a mixed model.

Future developments in ecclesial ministry will probably employ the language of catechesis. It is the more common ministerial term, presently used in those liturgical and pastoral documents that go beyond the scope of catechesis, such as in the *Rite of Christian Initiation of Adults.* Catechesis implies a community focus that is the basis for ministry. This focus is in keeping with the history of ecclesial catechetical activity, going back to the first few centuries of the church's life. Religious education does not have the same depth or richness of meaning.

Therefore, parishes may choose to model this shift to catechesis by replacing the language of religious education with appropriate catechetical language on all levels of parish ministry and organizational life. This language reflects recent developments in ministry and stresses the unique ministry of catechesis.

With the emergence of new pastoral ministries, responsibilities formerly given to parish catechetical personnel may be carried out more properly by other parish ministers. This changing climate requires a refocusing of catechetical ministry. This means that catechetical ministry becomes more limited in scope and that systematic catechesis, employing the catechetical process, takes on more importance. Consequently, catechetical personnel remember that their chief responsibility is catechesis and not counseling, service projects, ministry to senior citizens or divorced people, liturgy, or other ministries.

More limited responsibilities of catechetical personnel presume a well-developed model of parish ministry and a good working spirit between parish ministers. It is especially important to detail, in a job description, the specific functions of catechetical personnel. The catechetical staff should know how they relate to the overall catechetical plan of the parish. For this to happen, the parish develops a manageable model for working with the catechetical leaders, parents, catechists, and other ministers.

Finally, catechetical personnel know clearly the services they are expected to provide. This is especially important when new parish ministries develop. For example, if catechetical personnel concentrate on systematic catechesis and work closely with liturgical ministers, this affects the responsibility catechetical personnel assume in relation to sacramental preparation. If catechists are responsible for providing the catechesis involved in preparation for the sacraments, parish liturgists should assume similar responsibilities for liturgical preparation. Such changes in focus may necessitate a shift in parish ministerial responsibilities. The same applies if catechetical personnel concentrate on systematic catechesis in youth or family ministry, or in ministry to people with disabilities. It is also necessary to spell out the catechist's responsibilities in the RCIA processes. Catechetical leaders, and other parish leaders, clarify how catechists minister with the parish liturgist, sponsors, welcomers, and ministers of service.

The Vision of Catechesis

Parishes develop a vision of catechesis that is rooted in the kingdom and based on the parish's uniqueness. This is family-centered and holistic, integrating the chief ministries of word, worship, and service. All parish ministries blend these three ministries into an authentic response to individual needs.

To view a parish as a community of smaller communities that gather to celebrate the liturgy helps one see the flexibility needed to catechize various parish segments. In this catechetical endeavor, the smaller communities maintain contact with the wider parish, while catechists concentrate on the catechetical needs of the individual groups.

Each parish needs a well-articulated vision of catechesis to ensure ministry to all parishioners.

Suggestions for Parish Catechetical Ministry

The following recommendations follow from the previous study of parish catechetical ministry. They are divided into overall perspectives, parish, and parish catechesis.

Overall Perspectives

Evangelization is seen from a dialogical perspective. The three poles of this dialogue are: world (marketplace, culture, school, friends), family, and parish.

The evangelization/conversion process, with catechesis as one element, happens in the interplay of world, family, and church. Each contributes to the manifestation of the Good News. This implies that God communicates to humans through the family and the world. A parish catechist does not bring the Word to a person devoid of God's prior communication. The manifestation of the kingdom of God comes through life itself—family, friends, marketplace, culture, school, and work. The catechist illumines this presence through the Scriptures, church teaching, and Christian life.

Therefore, family and world, like church, are subjects of evangelization. They mutually enrich one another. When this subjective dialogue happens, the Good News remains alive and dynamic. In particular, the Church offers to this dialogue a vision of the kingdom as revealed by Jesus and taught by Christian tradition. This vision, in turn, leads to acts of service and celebration with the family and the world.

Parish

The parish acknowledges itself as a partner in the evangelization process, especially as parish relates to family. The term *family* includes integral, single-parent, and divorced families, as well as freely chosen friends bonded in a familial setting. In catechetical ministry, it is critically important to recognize these various groupings and to avoid advertising, programming, lectures, workshops, and preaching which presuppose that all families are integral or nuclear.

The parish and individual families must communicate. If either party fails to listen or respond, thus abrogating the responsibility of a partner, little communication results. From the parish perspective, certain elements recommend themselves to ensure reciprocity with family and world, necessary for effective evangelization and catechesis.

Welcome People need to feel at home in a parish. This applies to regular parish members and visitors alike. It is especially important during transition periods, such as birth, death, marriage, divorce, adolescence, and young adulthood. Many people going through a divorce feel parish support; others feel shunned. Today, youth frequently comment that they do not really feel welcome in their parish, that what happens there is for adults and children, and not for them.

Ministry begins with hospitality. The welcoming community lays the groundwork for further evangelization, catechesis, and celebration. Without hospitality, ministerial efforts often languish and suffer.

Centrality of Family Parishes must acknowledge the centrality of the family. Without this sensitivity, family life suffers. Consequently, family-oriented parishes treat the family as the subject, not the object, of the evangelization/conversion process. This means helping families with spiritual needs—including home catechesis, prayers, and devotions—as well as with the demands of society and work. Family-oriented parishes place top commitment on parish-as-family, including singles, rather than parish-as-institution, and limit the responsibilities family members are asked to assume in parish ministry.

When parishes see the family as the subject rather than the object of evangelization, ministerial efforts shift. The need to focus on the family also brings out

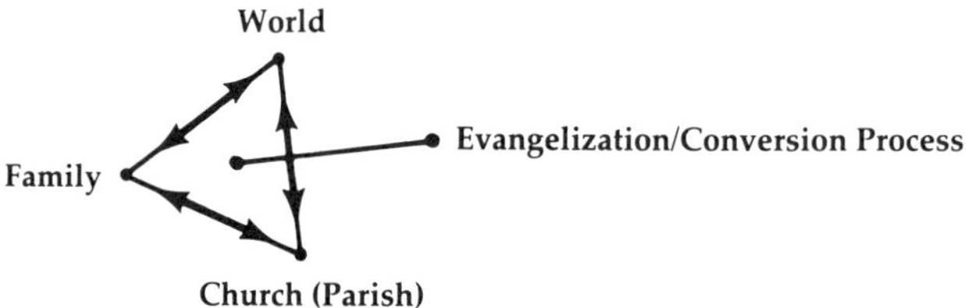

the importance of affirming single people and of providing the support systems that give them life. The centrality of family does not minimize the single life. Single people are members of a family. Every parish includes many unmarried people; efforts must be made to link them with the wider community.

Parish as Network of Communities No parish is a homogenous mass of people. Children, youth, young adults, parents, singles, divorced, senior citizens, ethnic and economic diversity, clubs, organizations, neighborhoods, and prayer groups are a few of the natural groupings in every parish. These need to be acknowledged, for diversity strengthens a parish. To tap into the gifts inherent in diversity requires an open style of leadership and clear direction. Without direction, diversity becomes confusion; with it, diversity brings creativity and new life.

At worship, in catechesis, and through service, parishioners celebrate unity in Christ and with each other, while acknowledging that cooperative people make possible an effective Christian community.

Mutuality of Ministries Parish ministries acknowledge the various gifts in a parish as the basis for ministry. From the beginning, the Christian church has acknowledged the Spirit of the risen Lord ministering through the gifts of the various members of the Body of Christ.

Effective catechesis, strengthened by a mutuality of ministries, is most effective when people minister to one another and see their call to minister as rooted in the Christian community. This ministry is celebrated in all the sacraments, especially in the rites of Christian initiation. People become aware of their call to minister in the ordinary experiences of life, and grow in this awareness by ministering to others in times of sickness, divorce, loss of job, or death.

To ensure effective collaborative ministries, parish leaders—including priests, catechetical leaders, catechists, and parish ministers—work together for a common purpose centered in the kingdom of God. The pastor is the key, even though effective parish growth occurs when the community is renewed together. As this happens, calling forth local leadership is crucial.

Effective parish ministry also means good catechesis is complemented by good liturgy, and vice versa, with ministerial service as the outgrowth of listening to and celebrating God's word. For this to happen, a parish needs constantly to prioritize and redirect efforts toward ministry to all groups within its membership.

Diverse Parish Styles While looking to the multiple challenges in parish ministry, the need to acknowledge diverse parish styles must be underlined. If the uniqueness of each parish is not affirmed, ministerial efforts may be largely ineffective.

Parish Life in the United States lists six styles of parish life: organization, hospitality, formation/evangelization, social action, service, and culture carriers. Each parish needs to ask what combination of these styles best reflects its orientation. Catechetical activities are always most effective to the degree that they link with the real parish situation.

Reexamine "Meetings" The stress on democratic decision making has multiplied meetings. Many people are "meeting-ed out." While desiring to serve, they often sense that little is accomplished at meetings. Parishes might reexamine the number and fruitfulness of meetings they ask people to attend.

Perhaps the time has come to look critically at what really must be handled at meetings and what can just as well be decided by administrators. People should be asked to attend meetings only if the meetings are necessary and well prepared. If the work can be done without a meeting, opt for this. Under the guise of planning, many busy adults are deprived of needed leisure time with families and loved ones because of parish meetings that often produce few results.

Good meetings are necessary for open leadership and can generate new vision, motivation, and ministry. A clearer distinction between policy-making meetings, advisory committees, and administrative decisions and actions leads to more fruitful meetings. People can easily experience confusion and frustration when many items discussed are more properly staff considerations or administrative matters. Catechetical leaders ought to reexamine the value of the meetings they ask parents, single people, and catechists to attend. Today, parishes need fewer but better meetings.

Parish Catechesis

Catechesis flows from parish life. Based on the parish perspective described in the previous chapter, certain conclusions apply specifically to catechetical ministry.

Return to the simple message of the Gospels. The number of Catholics, especially youth, who regularly attend or join fundamentalist Christian churches is a cause for concern on the part of sensitive ministers and parents. Some who leave the Catholic Church wonder if they are welcome and wanted. They often claim that the Church's message and structures are too complicated to meet their needs. On the other hand, they speak of discovering the simplicity of Jesus' message in fundamentalist churches.

While some may be making excuses, others feel it is necessary to leave the Catholic Church to discover Jesus. Whatever their reasons for leaving, the fact remains that their exodus presents a challenge to the Church. Their response points to the need for the Catholic community to take a look at the way parishes convey Jesus' message.

Complex doctrines and structures may be useful for theological clarification and church management, but they do little to move hearts toward conversion. Unless the Church relates all doctrines and structures to the goal of proclaiming the simple message of the Gospel, these doctrines and structures will have little impact on people's lives. Consequently, the Church needs to maintain a proper balance in its doctrines and structures, never forgetting that it exists to be an evangelizing community.

To teach as Jesus did means grounding his message in the life experiences of the persons being catechized. One does not have to be a fundamentalist to share the simple message of Jesus.

We receive help from Jesus himself in simplifying the Christian message and revitalizing our parish communities. He emphasized ministry to the poor, the alienated, and the sinner. Jesus found fault with those aspects of his Jewish tradition which had become too complex. But he never condemned or abandoned Judaism itself. Jesus' example teaches an important lesson.

The Christian community must always focus on the simple message of Jesus and allow it to speak for itself. To relate the Church's message and organizational structures to the simple message of the Gospel is not to disparage theology or minimize the need for organization. Solid pastoral theology and catechesis, however, should be readily understandable. Otherwise, the message that Jesus teaches us in his life of love may be too easily clouded in the complexities of rhetoric. The professional theologian exercises a valuable ministry by building upon the pastoral experience of today and relating the Church's great theological systems, magisterial statements, and history of doctrines to the present scene. As far as church structures are concerned, Jesus' teaching invites us to be constantly on guard lest the evangelical spirit of the gospels is lost in a maze of bureaucracy. When church structures become too complex, the Christian community is challenged to clarify the degree to which the spirit of the gospels permeates them.

Applying the evangelization/conversion process to church organizations is difficult. It is a tremendous challenge for the Catholic Church—universal, national, diocesan, or parochial—to put into institutional practice the challenges Pope Paul VI presents in *On Evangelization in the Modern World*. The degree to which the Church evangelizes its institutions is a positive indication of the seriousness with which Pope Paul's words are taken.

The need to simplify applies also to catechesis. The catechist is not primarily a theologian. To catechize as if catechesis means teaching a minicourse in theology does not accomplish the aims of catechesis. Catechesis speaks of the relationship between the Good News and life. When people claim that catechesis is too complex, boring, or uninspiring, one might question what is going on. The word of God is alive and speaks to all times and experiences. The truths of faith, when taught simply and vibrantly, have the power to evangelize and catechize. It is tragic to hear people say they do not hear the Good News in the Catholic Church because catechesis is too complex, homilies are impersonal, and hearts are not touched.

Quality Catechesis Parishes should stress quality over quantity in all ministry, including catechesis. This may necessitate a shift in priorities and responsibilities. To ensure quality catechesis, parishes

- emphasize catechist preparation;
- develop continuity in catechetical programs, emphasizing systematic catechesis and the catechetical process;
- plan ahead to ensure effective catechesis on all levels;
- maintain a commitment to keep qualified catechetical leaders—professional and volunteer—on the parish staff;
- provide clear job descriptions for all catechetical personnel;
- pay a just salary and benefits to catechetical personnel;
- afford an adequate budget for parish catechetical activities;
- maintain a catechetical library, including audiovisuals;
- provide sufficient space for catechetical sessions;
- develop good personal and professional support systems for catechetical personnel;
- link catechetical ministry with ministries of celebration, service, and community building; and

- help those responsible for catechesis to see the importance of balancing play, prayer, work, and solitude.

In addition, parishes need to provide catechetical opportunities for people of all ages and backgrounds. This demands a coordinated catechetical plan, centering on adults, but recognizing the importance of child and youth catechesis, and verifying the spirit of the kingdom in parish catechetical ministry through concern for the poor and those people with disabilities.

Community Responsibility for Catechesis The community (family, parish, school, and diocese) is the chief source of all ministry, including catechetical ministry. Here, the risen Lord shares his gifts for ministry. These gifts exist in the entire Body, not in one segment alone. The success of systematic catechesis is influenced by the attitude of the entire community.

The parish catechetical leader, catechists, or diocesan catechetical staff alone cannot control the ministerial spirit, including the attitude toward catechesis present in the wider community. Experiences in parishes and diocesan offices since Vatican II have made this clear. Nor is it the primary responsibility of catechetical leaders to do so. When the community works together to effect a vibrant ministerial spirit, catechesis comes alive. Until this happens, catechetical efforts are tentative.

A vibrant ministerial spirit encourages catechesis on all age and faith levels. To accomplish this, parish leaders—especially catechetical leaders and catechists—recognize that the family provides the groundwork for effective catechesis. Religious values begin to develop here. Consequently, family ministry must be a priority. Parishes need to help, not hinder, families through community activities and the responsibilities they give to parishioners. Family ministry is not furthered when parents, ministering to others in the name of the Church, spend too much time away from their families.

When catechists see that the entire community is responsible for informal catechesis, it becomes easier for them to concentrate on systematic catechesis and to see the limits of their ministry.

Catechetical Leadership Formation Success of catechetical ministry depends largely on the quality of catechetical leaders that parishes and dioceses call forth. Although the primary responsibility for catechetical ministry rests in the entire community, catechetical leaders are necessary to bring forth the community's gifts. Parishes and dioceses need to support existing catechetical leaders and encourage new leadership patterns.

Every community identifies and helps train catechetical ministers. But since parishes have different needs, they also require different catechetical styles. On a parish level, motivating and training catechists is essential. Some parishes have the resources to train their own catechists. But since the parish is part of a larger church community, the diocese also has responsibilities for catechetical training and for establishing standards for the formation and certification of catechists and catechetical leaders. The diocesan catechetical office may take an indirect role in catechist formation by approving and promoting catechist formation sessions on the local level, and a more direct role in the formation of catechetical leaders and master catechists who conduct such courses. Catechetical training can also be realized through diocesan personnel, workshops, and organizational endeavors. Parishes often do not have the resources to train catechists.

In a diocese, catechetical centers or sessions supplement parish catechetical training. The diocesan catechetical office assists parishes and provides opportunities which individual parishes cannot afford. Diocesan catechetical training concentrates on working with catechetical leaders and catechists, helping them to minister more effectively. In no instance does the diocese substitute for what should happen on the local level, or impose its own standards, failing to be sensitive to the catechetical needs of individual parishes.

The need to develop leadership means that the parish has a serious responsibility to inspire, encourage, and see that catechists are prepared. This is a special responsibility of parish catechetical leaders. In addition to other duties, these leaders implement diocesan policies and standards so as to develop effective parish catechesis. Diocesan responsibility revolves around working with parish and school catechetical leaders and catechists to help them perform their ministry more effectively. On a parish and diocesan level, this implies that regular sessions be held to encourage and develop trained catechetical leaders and catechists.

Collaborative Ministry Pastoral ministry is built upon a team model, where interlocking ministries serve the one mission of Christ. To be effective, this necessitates a close working together of various ministers to assess needs, establish priorities, and set goals and objectives. In many places, it also requires reorganization of parish and diocesan structures.

As this happens, catechists realize that catechesis is not an end in itself, but serves the mission of Christ and the Church. It flowers into service of others and celebration of the Lord's presence in life and liturgy.

Catechists work with other ministers to develop strong community support for ministry. They concentrate on the catechetical dimensions of their ministries. Even though the catechetical process includes liturgical and service aspects, the catechist is not expected to be an expert liturgical or service minister.

Strong relationships should exist between catechists and school personnel. Catholic schools are one way that the Church catechizes. In many parishes and dioceses, more adequate organizational relationships may have to be established between catechetical and school personnel, and between catechists and liturgical, youth, family, and other parish and diocesan ministers.

Focus of Catechetical Ministry With the development of ministries in the Church and the growing cooperation between ministers, catechists need to concentrate on their primary responsibility, namely, systematic catechesis. The form it takes varies, but the catechist focuses on the conversion and formational aspects of this ministry.

Since catechesis is an aspect of the evangelization process, "catechesis must often concern itself not only with nourishing and teaching the faith, but also with arousing it unceasingly with the help of grace, with opening the heart, with converting, and with preparing total adherence to Jesus Christ on the part of those who are still on the threshold of faith" (*Catechesi Tradendae,* 19). Catechists recognize the close relationship between catechesis and evangelization. Within the context of evangelizing activity, catechesis finds its proper place in the Church's pastoral and missionary activity.

Catechesis and Human Needs Good catechesis is sensitive to individual and community needs and takes into account that spiritual conversion, a lifelong process, acknowledges that the Lord comes to people in the many circumstances of life. Catechesis is part of this conversion process which begins at birth and lasts a person's entire lifetime. Consequently, opportunities for systematic catechesis should be available on every level of life, especially on the adult level.

Catechesis happens within the context of a person's life situation. This implies, for example, that systematic youth catechesis is linked with total youth ministry, with the catechist responsible only for the catechetical dimension of youth ministry.

Good catechesis can never omit the fact that faith is a gift from God. Neither solid content nor good methodology alone brings a person to the faith, but effective catechetical methods help people discover God's gift of faith as it relates to their life experiences.

Catechists are sensitive to the evangelizing, cultural, and ecumenical dimensions of ministry, and adapt their content and methods accordingly. At times, systematic catechesis takes an evangelizing approach, especially with children and youth, while all catechesis strives to educate for justice, which is a central aspect of Jesus' teaching ministry.

Finally, catechists teach in the name of the Christian community. They echo the Church's teaching, not merely theological opinions or personal insights. Catechesis is not primarily concerned with theological speculation, but with telling the Christian story from the perspective of faith. When theological issues arise, however, catechists distinguish clearly the official teaching of the Church from theological opinions or personal insights that differ from that teaching.

For Further Reflection

1. Is it time for your parish to reevaluate the number and quality of meetings?
2. What, in your opinion, are the significant points necessary for quality catechesis?
3. How does catechetical ministry in your parish fit within a collaborative ministerial model? Is it an essential component of youth ministry, the Catholic school, adult catechesis, and so on? If not, why not?
4. What are the most pressing catechetical needs in your parish? Rank them in order of priority.
5. What do you see as the future of catechetical ministry in your parish? What are some specific ideas that will make that vision a reality?

CONCLUSION

As parishes strive to bring the kingdom message to a changing culture, so does catechesis look to new and creative challenges. These challenges come from without and within. Challenges from without invite catechists to apply the message of the Scriptures to an undefined future, where people of different ages, backgrounds, and nations become one in their common concern for survival, justice, compassion, and peace. Challenges from within invite the parish community to simplify its message, take a look at its priorities, call all Christians to minister, and give a deep commitment to catechesis.

Catechesis is an important ministry, but one that does not stand on its own. It flows into liturgical celebration and is directed toward service. When this happens, church ministries become a harmonious picture.

As this happens, parish catechists learn they are imperfect people, cotravelers on a pilgrim journey. Catechists make mistakes, encounter imperfect parish structures, and discover pastoral ministers with whom they disagree. But, as people of faith, striving to minister within a broader community, catechists are blessed because they have responded to the Lord's call, "Come, follow me."

Parish catechesis is the right and responsibility of all parishioners. When Christians accept this responsibility, catechetical ministry bears fruit.